MARTIAL

MARTIAL

THE MAKING OF
MANCHESTER UNITED'S
NEW TEENAGE SUPERSTAR

LUCA CAIOLI
and
CYRIL COLLOT

Translated from the Italian and the French
by Laura Bennett

ICON

Published in the UK and USA in 2016
by Icon Books Ltd, Omnibus Business Centre,
39–41 North Road, London N7 9DP
email: info@iconbooks.com
www.iconbooks.com

Sold in the UK, Europe and Asia
by Faber & Faber Ltd, Bloomsbury House,
74–77 Great Russell Street, London WC1B 3DA or their agents

Distributed in the UK, Europe and Asia
by Grantham Book Services,
Trent Road, Grantham NG31 7XQ

Distributed in Australia and New Zealand
by Allen & Unwin Pty Ltd, PO Box 8500,
83 Alexander Street, Crows Nest, NSW 2065

Distributed in South Africa
by Jonathan Ball, Office B4, The District,
41 Sir Lowry Road, Woodstock 7925

Distributed in India by Penguin Books India,
7th Floor, Infinity Tower – C, DLF Cyber City,
Gurgaon 122002, Haryana

Distributed in Canada
by Publishers Group Canada,
76 Stafford Street, Unit 300, Toronto, Ontario M6J 2S1

Distributed in the USA
by Publishers Group West,
1700 Fourth Street, Berkeley, CA 94710

ISBN: 978-178578-097-4

Typeset in New Baskerville by Marie Doherty

Printed and bound in the UK by Clays Ltd, St Ives plc

About the authors

Luca Caioli is the bestselling author of *Messi, Ronaldo, Neymar, Suárez* and *Balotelli*. A renowned Italian sports journalist, he lives in Spain.

Cyril Collot is a French journalist. He is the author of several books about the French national football team and Olympique Lyonnais. Nowadays he works for the OLTV channel, where he has directed several documentaries about football.

Contents

1   Soaring towers   1

2   In the footsteps of Henry and Evra   9

3   The meeting   17

4   Between Manchester and Lyon   23

5   Discovering a new world   31

6   Already at national level   39

7   The new baby *gone*   45

8   Welcome to the pros   53

9   5 million euros   59

10   Regrets   65

11   Toto and the tsars   73

12   Cloudy skies over Monaco   81

13   Punishment   91

14   The click   99

15   A busy summer   109

16   The longest day   117

17   Anthony who?   127

18   A fairy-tale start   133

19   Wembley, 17 November 2015   143

20   A Christmas present   151

21   Goals, gossip and love stories   159

22   Anthony *Le Magnifique!*   167

23   Back home   179

24   Missed   185

A career in figures   191

Bibliography   193

Acknowledgements   197

Chapter 1
Soaring towers

'Why are the people who live in Les Ulis so surprised by the Bergères Towers? Why do they always ask why sixteen-storey buildings have been placed so close together when there is so much space around them?' The answer offered by a welcome pamphlet distributed to new arrivals is simple: 'The architects had no choice. They had to fit 10,000 homes on 200 hectares, not a handful of detached houses scattered across a park.'

Anthony Martial grew up in one of the soaring Bergères Towers, white, grey and pale coffee-coloured high-rise blocks that sprout up side by side in the centre of Les Ulis. We are twenty kilometres south east of Paris, in the *département* of Essonne, Île-de-France. On 17 February 2017, Les Ulis, caught between the A10 motorway and the 118 trunk road, will celebrate the first 40 years of its existence.

The story of Les Ulis began in 1960, when a ministerial decree authorised the urbanisation of an area between the towns of Bures-sur-Yvette and Orsay. It was intended to house employees, managers and researchers working for the Atomic Energy Commission, the large companies at the Courtabœuf business park, and the Université Paris Sud. In 1965, work started on the grassy fields used at that time for cultivating wheat, beetroot, strawberries and vegetables. France was experiencing a time of pronounced economic growth and improved living conditions during the period that would come to be known as the *Trente Glorieuses*. Robert Camelot, François Prieur and Georges-Henri Pingusson, the urban planners who designed Les Ulis, were inspired by the ideas of Le Corbusier: housing complexes, squares designed as terraces, internal streets for shops, and the separation of traffic flow, with walkways for pedestrians and streets for cars. It was a raised or elevated form of urban planning, an architecture of growth found in suburbs all over France. In 1968, the new development's first inhabitants moved into the Bathes and Courdimanche districts, although some buildings were yet to have running water. Eight years later, on 14 March 1976, the citizens of Bures-sur-Yvette, Orsay and the new town were called upon to choose between three proposals in a referendum: maintaining the status quo, the current administrative situation at that time; opting for Bures-sur-Yvette and Orsay to be merged to encompass Les Ulis; or creating a new, third commune called Les Ulis. The winner, by a very slim margin, was the third option, and, on 17 February 1977, the 196th commune of Essonne, Les Ulis, officially came into existence. Once again, the welcome pamphlet explains that its name 'comes from the Latin verb "*uller*", which means "to burn". The name of the town is derived from the ground on which stubble was burned to make fertiliser.'

In March 1977, Paul Loridant, a 28-year-old socialist, was elected mayor. His mandate would be renewed six times: he spent 31 years governing the town. The former Banque de France employee and one time senator for the Mouvement républicain et citoyen is now 68 and currently the deputy mayor in charge of finance and social affairs.

He remembers: 'When I arrived, the town was a huge open-air construction site. There was still plenty of building to be done: the market, post office, town hall, the Boris

Vian cultural centre, but there were already 20,000 inhabitants, people from all over France who came to work elsewhere in the region, or in Paris.' Eighteen per cent of the inhabitants were back then, and still are, of foreign origin.

Portuguese, Moroccans, Algerians, Tunisians, immigrants from Sub-Saharan Africa (Mauritania and Mali), Réunion and the Antilles (Guadeloupe and Martinique in particular). The population grew rapidly until 1982, when the inhabitants of Les Ulis reached almost 29,000, but this was followed by a slow demographic decline and consequent decay. Today, the municipality is home to barely 25,000. The percentage of young people living in the town has also fallen significantly. Why? According to Paul Loridant, the unresolved problem with Les Ulis is the integration and social evolution of a population of humble origins: 'We have not been able to stop people leaving when their standard of living improves and they start climbing the social ladder. They prefer to move to neighbouring towns, such as Orsay or Limours, or closer to Paris, where they think they will have a better life, where society is more mixed. In Les Ulis, where we have more than 50 per cent social housing, those who leave are replaced by new immigrants.'

Not everyone agrees with this view. Many mention social problems, delinquency and crime. 'This isn't the Bronx,' replies an indignant Benoît. 'This is a quiet town. It's nothing like some of the other towns around here. In 2005, during the *banlieue* riots, nothing happened here. There weren't any clashes or raids.'

'Difficult neighbourhoods? No, there aren't any,' confirms Yassine. 'Everyone knows everyone here and we respect one another.' We're half an hour from Paris and we have plenty of advantages without any of the inconvenience.

This is a cosmopolitan town that produces rappers and footballers, nothing else.' But the local newspapers talk of drug
trafficking, cannabis in particular. They say that Les Ulis
has ended up on the *liste rouge* of problem towns and cities.
They report incidents between youths and the police, as in
the summers of 2009 and 2015. Paul Loridant admits: 'Yes,
there have been incidents, but never anything serious and
certainly no more than in other cities in the Paris *banlieue*.'
As any good administrator would, the deputy mayor stresses
the positive steps taken in terms of culture and infrastruc-
ture. He talks about kids from seriously underprivileged
families in Les Ulis who have gone on to become university
professors and leading researchers. Above all, he illustrates
the current redevelopment, a genuine reconstruction to
adapt the town to the demands of modern life. An ambitious project to revamp a style of urban planning that has
failed to stand the test of time. A stroll around the city
centre near the town hall, esplanade and market is all it
takes to grasp that this is a place undergoing a transforma-
tion. Beneath the low-flying aircraft coming in to land on
runways three and four at the nearby Paris Orly airport,
they are working everywhere you look to change the face
of Les Ulis. They are even re-cladding the towers. 'That
one there, at the bottom, near the park, the Tour Janvier,
that's where Anthony lived,' says Jean Paul. He points to
a sixteen-storey high-rise block like all the others, named
after the months of the year and separated by gardens and
leafless trees.

Born fifteen kilometres from here, in Massy, on
5 December 1995, Anthony is the third son of Florent and
Myriam. His father comes from Le Gosier in Grande-Terre,
Guadeloupe; he was born there in 1962. Florent came to
metropolitan France at the age of twenty for his military

service with the navy in Brest. After finishing his national service he stayed in France for two and a half years. It was then that he met Myriam, his future wife, who was also from Guadeloupe, from Petit-Bourg in Basse-Terre. Florent went back to Guadeloupe for six months but returned in 1985 to settle once and for all on the mainland. The couple married in 1986 and then moved to the Paris region. 'We came to Les Ulis in 1988,' remembers Florent Martial. 'It was a young town, expanding towards Paris, near the motorways. I was working at the prefecture; my wife was working for a pharmaceutical company. Dorian, our first child, was born in 1989, followed by Johan in 1991 and then Anthony. We lived in Le Bosquet [another part of Les Ulis] and the kids all slept in the same room. Then, when Anthony was three, we moved into the Bergères Towers and they all had their own room. Of course, it was hectic at home with three boys. But they were good kids and they always felt understood. They were close as brothers. What was Anthony like? He didn't like to be bothered. Whenever he looked at you out of the corner of his eye, that said it all. He was a bit reserved, he didn't say much and he only smiled when he wanted to. He was very calm and collected.'

'My brother has always had a strong character, perhaps the strongest of the three of us,' explains Dorian, the eldest who now lives about thirty kilometres from Les Ulis and works as a technician on fire detection systems. 'He was stubborn and there was trouble almost every day but that's normal among brothers. Anthony is a kind person, although at school, in his own little world, he didn't like to be annoyed.'

'I met him at the École Primaire du Parc when we were six. We went to junior school together, then two or three years at secondary school. He was hyperactive in the classroom and a bit unruly. You could see that studying wasn't for him. He was clever. He worked but didn't want to spend hours with his nose in a book. He wanted to spend them with a football. I remember he was already very good when he was little. He was the only kid in Year 2 who played with the kids in Year 6. He would take free kicks like Roberto Carlos, with his left foot, even though he's right-footed. Who were his idols? Ronaldo, the Brazilian Ronaldinho, and Zidane. He supported Olympique Lyonnais, the team that was winning everything in France back then. But he also liked Guardiola's Barcelona. The first shirt he had was Sonny Anderson, the Brazilian striker for Les Gones [OL's nickname, meaning 'The Kids' in Lyon's regional dialect],' remembers Fabrice Tenin, nicknamed Pépère. With his brother Baptiste, nicknamed Titoune, Pépère was one of Anthony's best friends.

'The Tenins were our neighbours in Les Ulis,' remembers Florent Martial. 'Anthony was always at their house. Mimose, their mother, thought of him as one of her own. She would cook his favourite dinner, chicken. Still now, even though we don't live in Les Ulis anymore, whenever he comes back to Paris, Anthony almost always goes to see her first.'

'Life's changed today. The city's changed and society's changed,' continues Tenin. 'We have generation 3.0 now, PlayStations and mobile phones, but when we were small, we had a ball. We never stopped playing with it. We would spend whole days playing on the elevated section, on the cement walkways or on the little pitch down there below Anthony's tower. It was a grass pitch with goals and nets that were changed twice a year. Our parents could keep an eye on us and call us in for dinner from the window.'

Who taught Anthony to play football?

'His father and his older brothers. I would see them playing on Sundays sometimes, on the pitch under the tower.'

'Yes, it was our dad who passed on his passion for football to us,' explains Dorian. 'He played in an amateur team in Guadeloupe when he was young.'

'I was an attacking left winger for AS Gosier,' Florent confirms. 'I started playing when I was fourteen and stayed until I was twenty. I could have played in the CFA amateur league but then I left to do my military service.' He adds: 'In those days, I was a Marseille fan but now I support Troyes [the team in which Johan plays] and Manchester United.'

'I'm not surprised that he made it from Les Ulis to United. He's a chilled-out guy, quiet, with a great character. He hasn't let it go to his head. Last year', continues Tenin, 'I went to Manchester to visit him with Baptiste, my brother, and Anthony's parents to celebrate his twentieth birthday. I have to say, he hasn't changed a bit. He's still the same as he was when we played at school.

What has he left here in Les Ulis?

Françoise Marhuenda, Mayor of Les Ulis, explains: 'His success has given people courage. He passes his values on to young people and proves that anything is possible, that when you want something you can succeed. He's also passed on his sporting values: tenacity, respect, citizenship and fair play, everything that is also important in everyday life.'

'His example has undoubtedly had a positive impact. He's left a powerful mark,' Tenin concludes. 'Kids start playing football by following his example. But he's also left a legacy that will be hard to take on. So many dream of becoming like him, but there's only one Anthony.'

Chapter 2
In the footsteps of Henry and Evra

A big grey box next to the running track in the Stade Jean-Marc Salinier. Outside, on a dark winter's evening, it is cold and foggy, but right at the end of a synthetic pitch, beneath the floodlights, a group of children has just started training. Inside, a yellow light is on and people are constantly coming and going. Boys and girls with bags slung over their shoulders enter the brand new clubhouse, on their own or accompanied by fathers, mothers, brothers and sisters. They politely say '*Bonsoir*', shake hands with the directors, coaches and casual visitors before going to get changed in the dressing rooms next door. The club's first rule is to be courteous and behave properly, greeting everyone with a smile. 'They don't have to make an effort. They do it willingly. They're smart,' says Jean-Michel Espalieu, Vice-President of the Club Omnisport Les Ulis, Football Division.

Talking as he sits behind a long table, he is trying to look after a little girl who has no intention of sitting still, even for a second. The gaze of the person he is talking to shifts from the little girl, who has now gone in search of some coloured pencils, to the yellow walls: a gallery of memorabilia and a parade of champions. There's a white Manchester United shirt with the number 9, worn by Anthony Martial;

the number 14 *blaugrana* Barcelona shirt worn by Thierry Henry; and Patrice Evra's black and white striped number 33 Juventus shirt. These hang next to the club's blue and white flag, against which the colourful pennants of other clubs stand out: AS Poissy, Olympic Hallennois, PSG, Racing Club de Lens, Le Mans Union Club, Inter Milan and Borussia Dortmund. There are more shirts in blue frames: from Coulibaly to Johan Martial, from Sanogo to Evra's Manchester United shirt, and, at the end, Anthony's number 23 Monaco shirt. This is where the Manchester United striker began playing football seriously, here on Avenue des Cévennes in Les Ulis. An association formed at the same time as the town, in 1977, has since become the Club Omnisport. It now boasts 28 disciplines (from aikido to hockey, from archery to boxing) and 4,200 members. The lion's share of those are there for the football. 'We have 830 members, almost three per cent of the entire population of Les Ulis. We are the third largest club in Essonne,' explains Espalieu. 'Evry is the largest, with 1,200 members, but that's only two per cent of the town's inhabitants. Every category is represented: we go from the Under 6s to the veterans, from five-year-olds to 35-year-olds and beyond. We also have a women's section that's booming, with 45 ladies. From Under-6 to Under-11 level our club is considered one of the best in France, and not just by us. Three years ago we renovated this clubhouse, converted an old red clay pitch to synthetic and built another. Now, to accommodate all our players, we have a sports complex (two grass pitches, three synthetic pitches, an athletics track and twelve dressing rooms) that is in keeping with our ambitions.'

Besides their facilities, what marks the club out, they say around town, is its family feel and that it spends a significant amount of time working with local kids at grass roots level.

'We don't set technical priorities, we accept anyone at any time of year. What prevails here are educational and social goals. Our priority is to train the kids, to get them to have fun and stay away from the troubles of the *banlieue*,' says Mahamadou Niakaté, who interrupts his long conversation with an impeccably dressed broker on the other side of the table to have his say. Niakaté, aged 37, has been responsible for the football school since 1987, while also coaching the senior team and playing for the veterans. He insists: 'Just by way of an example, I can tell you that four years ago we had university tutors come to the club to help the kids who were struggling at school. Even if there are parents who enrol their kids believing that in the blink of an eye we'll transform them into champions capable of earning piles of money, we're not here to create professional footballers.' Whatever the case, the results of this instructional club speak for themselves: as well as Thierry Henry and Patrice Evra, its alumni include Yaya Sanogo (formerly at Arsenal and Crystal Palace, now at Charlton Athletic) and Jules Iloki (FC Nantes), to name only the most famous; more than ten youngsters from Les Ulis have gone on to become professional footballers. Henry, the former Gunners striker who had spells at Barcelona, Juventus and Monaco, France's all-time leading goal-scorer and now a commentator for Sky Sports, was born in Les Ulis in 1977 to West Indian parents, just like Anthony. He started playing at the club when he was six, before moving to US Palaiseau in a neighbouring town at the age of twelve. He has kept up his ties to the city and, with his One 4 All foundation, has contributed more than €200,000 to funding a seven-a-side synthetic pitch in the Bosquet neighbourhood.

'Patrice is a friend,' explains Niakaté, who played alongside both Henry and Evra. We know him better as a person than as a player. Although he was only with us for a season, he still helps us. He sponsored the senior team, bought strips and sports equipment and, when he was playing in the Premier League, he invited 40 of our kids to watch a game at Old Trafford. He also donated his bonus [€27,000] from the 2010 World Cup, which was marred by the players' revolt in Knysna.'

Neither Henry nor the France and Juventus defender spent a great deal of time on the club's pitches, unlike Anthony; it is obvious the directors have a weakness for the kid from the Bergères Towers. It is clear for all to see in the team photos from when Martial was about seven, or the little shrine dedicated to him with the front page of *L'Équipe* of 25 September 2015 on display. It shows a full-page photo of the number 9 with the title '*Épatant Martial* [Stunning Martial]' and a paragraph that recalls:

'The French striker whose record transfer was so controversial has a thundering start to the season. Four goals in four games for Manchester United and a popularity rating that is already sky-high in England.'

No one in Les Ulis has forgotten the first few weeks of that September. 'It was the only thing we were talking about here, and everyone was following the story minute by minute on tablets, phones, Facebook, social networks and websites,' confesses Aziz Benaaddane, the technical director and Under-17 coach who joins in the conversation after arriving late. 'I have to say that we weren't particularly surprised by the news of his transfer. We're used to seeing our kids go to big teams. What we were struck by was the amount United paid. Although I'm convinced the boy is worth it and is a great investment for the future.'

Value judgements aside, they were intense days for the club. It was literally stormed by the French media. When they found out about the figures involved, troops of reporters arrived from anywhere and everywhere. It was a frenzy. Cars and vans from radio and TV companies invaded the car park. The directors' mobile phone voicemails were clogged with requests for interviews from Norway to Japan.

'We responded to everyone. We must have given more than 50 interviews and even ended up live on the *TF1* news,' remember Niakaté, who was struck by the curiosity of the English media who turned up on the first Eurostar. 'We were still here at the stadium at ten o'clock at night speaking to them, and the next morning I found them outside my house as they were going to Anthony's old junior school. They wanted to know absolutely everything about Martial's life.' They were keen to learn as much as possible about the Golden Boy. They were also curious to know how Les Ulis would use the €250,000 it would get from Martial's transfer, as the club that trained him from age twelve to fourteen. It was a jackpot that was almost the equivalent of the annual budget of the club on Avenue des Cévennes. 'We bought four minibuses with the first €100,000 to give us some independence when playing away matches. We will invest the rest in new instructors, in their training, in educational materials and sports equipment. Nothing crazy. We don't recruit people at top dollar, none of our players has a federal contract [the equivalent of a professional contract for amateurs] and our first team staff also coaches the kids. We don't want to get ideas above our station,' says Benaaddane.

The €250,000 also made the Martial family happy. 'Les Ulis is a club that is close to our hearts,' Johan Martial told *Le Parisien* 'Our story started here and it's thanks to the club that we've come this far.'

'I'm happy that they'll get such a sum,' explained

Florent. 'The instructors here do a fantastic job. When he was younger Anthony could be a bit temperamental … But they looked after him.' They began looking after Anthony at Les Ulis in the autumn of 2001.

'Dorian was the most motivated of the three brothers. He wanted to play football and I took him to Les Ulis, then Johan followed. As his big brothers were playing, Anthony wanted to do the same and he started when he was five, a year before the minimum age group. With him it was all about football, he wasn't interested in other sports. I wouldn't say that he had anything special straight away. It was as time went on that we began to see his aptitude. From Under-11 tournaments and up,' Mr Martial senior explains.

'I always wanted to be a footballer. I never thought about doing anything else, it's what I've wanted from a very young age. I remember my very first training session,' recalls Anthony. 'It was raining heavily and it was cold. I trained for ten minutes and then I told my dad I wanted to go home.'

Niakaté, his coach, explains: 'No, I don't remember that first time but I haven't forgotten that he would come with his dad to watch his brothers' matches when he was tiny. He followed their example. Johan played here for two years before going to Paris Saint-Germain. Dorian still plays here, in the seniors. He's a great guy, a good defender, a number 5 that I sometimes put on the right wing even if it makes his father angry. He was never bothered about going to see the professional clubs, but he's still been successful. He's in love with the ball. He travels 30 kilometres a day to come to training.'

Benaaddane goes on to say: 'The Martials are simple, quiet people. It's never gone to their heads. When Johan signed for Brest they didn't go mad. And they haven't changed since Anthony signed his million euro contract.

They're not about the bling, fast cars or huge mansions. They did leave their apartment here in Les Ulis but they moved a few kilometres away to Saint-German-les-Corbeil, to a simple single-family house. Florent is a football fan. Often on Sundays he comes to watch Dorian's matches when he could be in the stands at Manchester United. The mother is a lovely, kind lady and, with a football-mad husband and three sons, she had no choice but to take an interest and she gradually started to like it. His mother and father gave Anthony a very strict upbringing because the boy could be temperamental.'

'Stubborn, determined, proud, shy, sometimes grumpy and very reserved. He was a child who didn't speak much around adults,' says Espalieu. 'He was much more expansive with his teammates though, he liked to joke and laugh. He was well-liked by everyone, which isn't easy because the best player in the team is not always popular. He was though. He was liked by those who played with him. They respected him for what he could do with the ball at his feet. And they stuck together. I'll tell you about the time when Anthony left his kit bag at home, with all the things he needed to have a shower. We told everyone that if they forgot it, they couldn't play. Martial shouldn't have been on the pitch for that game. But his teammates came to see me one after the other. Some offered to lend him soap, others shampoo or a towel. They knew it wouldn't be easy playing without him. So, we had to say OK then, but this is the last time.'

'At age six, most of the kids do "pre-training". They have fun, play, wander off to count four-leafed clovers around the pitch. Anthony was different,' explains Niakaté. 'He knew about football. He knew what a football was. He already had a good understanding of the basics, but he didn't give himself airs and graces,' remembers Wally Bagou, who had him for two years in the Under 7s and Under 13s. The instructor has just finished training the youngest children. He has come back to the clubhouse for a chat and to warm up. He sits down and says: 'On the pitch, he wanted to win at all costs and when his team lost he was uncontrollable. He would get angry and sulk but he wouldn't cry. He was tough. He was magnificent.'

'My first memory of Anthony? He must have been six,' remembers Benaaddane. 'He took the ball in his area and went on to score, leaving his opponents in his wake. We had 400 kids but a talent like him was rare.

'No one thought he would be a professional, a champion, but you could see from a mile away that he had some interesting qualities and great potential,' explains Niakaté. 'He reminded me of Henry: he was an intelligent goal-scorer, fast, elegant and decisive. We kept an eye on him. We tried to spur him on to get the best out of his potential.' And … let's just say they had to push him to work seriously because training and drills were not his forte. They were too much effort. But when it came to playing, he always had a smile on his face, thanks to the stimulus given by his instructors and his desire to improve, as well as a determined character and the talent of a child who took no time in making huge steps forward. He always jumped ahead to the next category: from the *débutants* (Under 7s) to the *poussins* (Under 11s), from the *poussins* to the *benjamins* (Under 13s). He always ended up playing with the bigger kids.

Chapter 3

The meeting

His name appeared at the bottom of the list, written in
pen in the eleventh position. It came after Hapt, Laidoi,
Benhassine, Zayed, Dieye, Grosy, Kabral Bissi, Bathily,
Azurmendi and Khouildi. The licence number was
2318054571. His date of birth was wrong: 30/12/1995. It
would have made him twenty-five days younger than he was.
Anthony was the only one born in 1995; his teammates were
born in 1993 or, like Deyne, Irwin, Tarek and Mousur, in
the first half of 1994. The list, which was filled out and given
to Nadine Bernard with the corresponding photographs,
was the Les Ulis B team registration form for the Tournoi
International Benjamins de Gif-sur-Yvette, an Essonne town
with 20,000 inhabitants, three and a half kilometres from
Les Ulis.

In 2004, the powers that be at OC Gif Football, the town's
sports club, came up with the idea of 'allowing children
from the region's clubs to enjoy an unforgettable experience as part of a festival of football,' to quote the tournament brochure. Although the event was limited to local
teams in its first year, in its second year, Philippe Renard,
the logistics manager, and Pierre Durand, responsible for the
technical side of the tournament, had bigger ambitions
and decided to extend participation to national and international clubs. Durand, then a recruiter for RC Lens,
invited friends and acquaintances to bring their teams to

the tournament, for boys aged between eleven and twelve. This appeal was answered by fifteen clubs from Essonne, six from Île-de-France, four from other *départements* and three professional clubs: Rennes (Ligue 1), Créteil and Reims (L2). But someone dropped out at the last minute and they needed to find a club to fill the final spot in the 32-team draw. 'I picked up the phone and called Aziz Benaaddane,' remembers Durand. 'I asked him if they could get a second team together to take part in our event.' The answer was yes, hence the Les Ulis B team list on which, aged barely nine and four months, Anthony Martial appears. He was two years below his category, *surclassé* as the French say. On 31 April and 1 May 2005, 500 children took part in the 'festival of football' at the Parc Municipal des Sports Michel Pelchat. Olympique de Saint-Étienne won the tournament, beating Evry in the final.

For Anthony Martial, who was well-known in Gif-sur-Yvette following matches between the two clubs, it was his first opportunity to see how he measured up at a national level, against boys who were much older than he was. But he was still small and they did not let him play a great deal. He made a good impression but failed to dazzle those watching. One year on and things could not have been more different. Now in its second year, the Gif Cup was held on Saturday, 29 and Sunday, 30 April 2006. Yves Invernizzi, the club's press officer, recalls: 'It was still modest and stuttering but it already included ten pro clubs (Lyon, Lens, Rennes, Bordeaux, Caen, Nice, Sochaux, Bastia, Reims and Créteil) and one foreign one, Servette from Geneva. This time Les Ulis only fielded one team, led by Mourad El Othmani. Anthony played as the number 10 and entered another world: he was taking on apprentice footballers from the best academies in France and playing against professional clubs. The first match was against Bordeaux and Les Ulis surprised with a 1-1 draw. In the final match, in the round of 16, they beat Nice 1-0, finishing seventh in a tournament won by the Centre de Formation de Football de Paris. It was quite a feat for an amateur club, one that attracted the attention of observers and scouts. Above all, they were curious about the exploits of the number 10, exploits he would keep repeating.

A taxi driver by profession, in 2006 Sébastien Torres was in charge of the youth section at FC Orsay Bures, a small club in Orsay, a town in Essonne. He remembers: 'We were supposed to play in a seven-a-side tournament in Marcoussis, a modest town near here better known for its rugby than its football. We didn't really know what we were going to come up against or how good the other teams would be. We wanted to involve all our kids, without exception, which was why our team was the weakest. We arrived in Marcoussis first thing in the morning. It was nearly winter and it was bitterly cold. It was raining cats and dogs and some of our kids were missing. We politely asked Mehdi, the Les Ulis coach, who we knew well, if he could lend us some players. No problem, he sent over two little kids to put on our purple shirts. We didn't have our first-choice keeper so we asked the two from Les Ulis if they would mind going in goal. Step forward Anthony Martial, who wasn't yet eleven. In the first match we lost with a score more suited to tennis. Mehdi came to watch and told us: 'Guys, please put him up front, not in goal!' For the second game, Anthony played up front and it was a revelation. He scored goal after goal and almost single-handedly sent us into the semi-final. It was huge. Just incredible. We couldn't believe it, with our team the way it was and the fact that we'd brought the kids to the tournament just to get some experience. Nor could we believe they'd lent us such a little gem. In the semi-final we lost 1-0 to Les Ulis, who had a team that was a hundred times better than ours. After the game, I went to see Mehdi and asked him: "Who's the phenomenon?" He laughed and answered: "He's the best striker in Île-de-France."'

On 12 and 13 May 2007, Anthony showed the same form in the third Tournoi International Benjamins de Gif-sur-Yvette. This time he was being watched by someone who would play a fundamental role in his career. 'I'd gone to watch the tournament because there were several professional clubs, from France and abroad. I was interested in seeing the second-year *benjamins* because I was an instructor at ACBB (AC Boulogne-Billancourt) and in charge of the Centre de Formation de Football Paris,' remembers Philippe Lamboley in his Paris office. 'I didn't know Anthony … but then I saw him play. He was a few months past his eleventh birthday. He was tiny and hadn't had any training but he made the difference. He could jump over three or four opponents with disarming ease and go on to score. Yes, that little kid playing for Les Ulis made a real impression on me. His parents and I had a mutual friend, Yannick Gadelle, who was working at the time as a recruiter for Bastia and had signed Johan Martial for the Corsican club. I asked him to put me in touch with the family. I went to see Anthony's parents and explained what I could do for the boy and how I could look after him and help him. I told them we would need to move quickly because Anthony would undoubtedly be the focus of interest from lots of professional clubs. I needed to warn them about what could happen, equip them so they would get the best possible result and the boy could stay calm and relaxed without anything interfering with his development. I told them about my plans and offered the family my help so they could make the best choice for the future. They trusted me. I became Anthony's agent and started looking after his career.' It was to be a dazzling career that progressed at lightning fast speed.

'When he was eleven we had to move him up a category. He was precocious and much further ahead of the others. He helped us win championships and cups. I remember he once even played two matches in a row. First, he won 4-0 with his team and then came back on the pitch with the Under 13s. At half time they were losing 2-0. He turned things around on his own and they won 3-2. In one year, from eleven to twelve, he had acquired power and improved his technique and vision of the game. He was the youngest member of the team but he was already the captain and leader. He didn't miss a single training session and even when he was away having a trial, he always made sure he didn't miss any sessions or matches. He played to have fun and would score twice in every game, 40 goals a season,' remembers Benaaddane, who trained him at Under-12 and Under-13 level. He adds: 'At twelve we were all convinced he was a star. We knew he would sign with some great clubs.'

Faced with ever increasing pressure and constant enquiries, Lamboley decided to take advantage of his contacts at Olympique Lyonnais. He had already taken Issiar Dia and Demba Ba to Lyon for trials. He was convinced the club would be a good choice for Anthony because its training centre had always produced great strikers and Lyon was a city where a quiet life was possible. He phoned Gérard Bonneau, who was responsible for recruitment at OL.

'Philippe worked with us as a recruiter in the Paris area and had told us about other youngsters. He knew about my weakness for good strikers. He called and told me: "I've seen a player you'll like. He's won me over. He's an unusual striker. A bit dozy, with his head in the clouds, but he's a great talent. Come and see him as soon as you can. Make it quick as lots of people are interested."' Bonneau recalls over a glass of Côtes du Rhône and a steak tartare in a restaurant next to the Stade de Gerland, the former home of OL: 'I trusted his eye and experience and I decided to go and see for myself.'

Chapter 4

Between Manchester and Lyon

'The first time I saw him was at Lyon station with his father. He was small, fragile, not very tall and like a little sparrow. He was introverted but his eyes twinkled. You could tell he wanted to come with us and, why not, to continue his adventure.' It was Easter 2008 and Olympique Lyonnais were taking their generation of players born in 1995 to Sens (Yonne), a town 100 kilometres from Paris, to compete in the Tournoi Sans Frontière. Founded in 1994, the event is for twelve-year-old boys and has witnessed the likes of Mavuba, Gonalons, Valbuena, Griezmann, Nasri, Ben Arfa, Kompany and Benzema.

The coach of the Les Gones team was Cyrille Dolce, who went to collect the new arrival at the station. 'Whenever we go to a new tournament we like to try out new players, from a footballing and sporting perspective as well as from a personality and behaviour angle,' explains Dolce, sitting on a bench in the dressing rooms at the Plaine des Jeux de Gerland as he waits for his current squad of Under-15 boys to arrive for their afternoon training.

'A three-day event like the one at Sens (21–23 March 2008) gives us the chance to see them live and play. There's time for us to form an opinion and confirm whether or not they will come to the club. Gérard Bonneau and his team had told us about a boy in Paris, at Les Ulis: Anthony Martial.'

Bonneau remembers: 'I had gone to see him at

Clairefontaine, where he had his first trial to be admitted to the Institut National de Football' [the Fédération Française de Football's talent factory that has produced Henry, Ben Arfa, Matuidi and Anelka]. 'What did I see in Martial? A boy who was asleep up front, sometimes he was there and sometimes he wasn't. But as soon as the ball came to him he knew how to play. He was attacking, had a real burst of speed and an impressive last-gasp lunge. And he was only twelve! You don't see many players like him at that age. He was unusual, with qualities all of his own and extra-ordinary strengths that reminded me of Karim Benzema, Bernard Lacombe, Cédric Bardon, Florian Maurice and Fleury Di Nallo, all OL's great goal-scorers. It was like a flash seeing him. A flash of Ronaldo Luís Nazário de Lima. Of course, I wouldn't have put my hand in the fire and sworn that he was going to become a great champion, at age twelve there are too many factors that can influence the development of a footballer, but I was certain of his potential. I was certain he could be a high-level athlete, so we decided to invite him for the Tournoi Sans Frontière.'

In Sens, OL finished fourth after losing 2-1 in the semi-final to Bayer Leverkusen and in the third place playoff against Lille. Anthony played in eight games for a total of 145 minutes and scored four goals: One against AS Saint-Étienne in the opening match, one against Borussia Dortmund and two against SK Slavia Prague.

Goals aside, how did that first tournament in the OL shirt go? 'Well, first of all, in terms of his personality. Anthony showed himself to be an interesting, polite, measured and discreet boy. You could sense he had a stable family behind him and parents who paid close attention to him. He came with humility and without any of the airs and graces of being "a big player from Paris." He had that West Indian "warmth" that made it easy for him to get close to people and win them over.' Dolce explains: 'Whenever a boy comes to us for a trial I like to see the match report. Whether they pass the ball to him or not, whether he inspires confidence in his teammates. Really, whether he has magnetism with the ball. All this means a lot to me. It means he has talent, something special that allows him to fit in perfectly with the group. I intentionally didn't put Anthony in his favourite position, that of an out-and-out striker. I played with a 4-3-3. I didn't want to depart from my tactics and we already had a quality striker. As far as I'm concerned, it's the player who has to fit in with the playing formation, not the other way around. I used him on the left wing, on his wrong foot, a bit like Thierry Henry. What struck me first was his apathy, his nonchalance. He gives you the impression he's playing with the handbrake on but it's just an illusion because when he wants to, he goes up a gear and into turbo drive. He has an easy touch on the ball that makes it look as if everything he's doing is simple. He is capable of making the difference at any moment, of dribbling tightly, of getting away from his marker quickly, of crossing from the left, of shaping up for a shot in a limited space and seeing it through with power and speed of execution. Despite playing him out of position, Anthony showed his class. He immediately developed a special relationship with his teammates and looked as if he was a Lyonnais player. He provided assists as well as scoring himself. At the end of the Sens tournament, we had no choice but to give him our stamp of approval,' Dolce concludes. 'He was an OL player. He had done more than enough to demonstrate it.'

How did Anthony feel after this trial? Just take a look at the tournament photograph. He is standing next to a bench marked with the word 'Sens'. His arms are behind his back in a schoolboy pose. He is smiling. He is happy and proudly showing off his red team sweatshirt, as if to say ' *Voilà, je suis à OL.* '

But it was to be another seventeen months before he arrived at the Lyon club. Seventeen very intense months. Martial continued to play for Les Ulis and to wreak havoc. He was tempted by Monaco and England and passed the selection process at Clairefontaine.

For Aziz Benaaddane and the other directors at Les Ulis, this was a period they will never forget. 'We were playing the semi-final of the Coupe de l'Essonne against ESA Linas-Montlhéry. It was the middle of winter and Anthony had spent the morning at Clairefontaine for a three-hour training session. By the time his father had brought him back to Les Ulis there were only twenty minutes of the match remaining. He quickly got changed behind the bench. With the permission of the referee, we brought him on. He scored with his first touch. We brought him off immediately so he could rest.' Benaaddane thinks for a moment and then adds: 'It was a shame they didn't take him at the Institut National de Football. He had passed the first, second and third tests and made it right to selection but they didn't pick him.'

Why not? André Merelle, who was in charge of the INF Clairefontaine for twelve years, offers this explanation: 'When we saw Anthony's report card we were concerned. We knew Lyon were interested in the boy and we thought he would still end up in good hands.'

'They said they didn't take him because of his results in the classroom,' Philippe Lamboley responds. 'I never heard anything about it and it turned out that when Anthony came to Lyon he didn't have any particular problems at school. But it was obvious that they brought up his grades and report cards because if they had excluded him for footballing reasons they would have made us look terrible. However, I have to say that the boy hasn't been too affected by that door slamming in his face.'

It may have been to do with his character, his nonchalance or because, as many had remarked, even at age thirteen he already had a good head on his shoulders, but the fact was that Anthony did not take no for an answer, just as he did not allow himself to become big-headed after a yes. Take what happened at Manchester City. When he was thirteen, City invited him to visit the club's facilities. He spent a week in England with his family. 'We liked it and we did think about it but in the end we decided to choose Lyon,' explains Florent Martial. 'It was more practical and Anthony had been a Lyonnais supporter since he was small.' Anthony was there with Adrien Rabiot, now a midfielder with PSG. Rabiot stayed and signed a six-year contract, although it did not go as planned for him and after six months he was back in France. Anthony and his family went home. Their trip to England had to remain a secret; few people knew about it and Anthony kept it to himself, but the news still reached the directors of Les Ulis. They were amazed to see him at his team training sessions as if nothing had happened: 'I had a trial at Manchester City, so what?'

City was not the only club interested in snatching up the phenomenon. 'Every weekend', remarks Niakaté, 'there was a line of recruiters from big clubs. Not one, not two, not three, but they all turned up. Half of Europe came to watch his matches, so much so that we became paranoid. We only had to spot someone walking their dog near the pitch and we thought they were a scout from one club or other.'

The boy from Les Bergères was courted by almost every team in France, starting with AS Monaco. Lamboley remembers: 'Dominique Bijotat, who was director of the Monegasque training centre at the time, came to the Martials' home with a document ready to be signed by Anthony's parents. I had to intervene: "What are you doing? We're definitely not here to sign a contract with Monaco."'

Gérard Bonneau was kept updated about all these advances by Lamboley and he decided there was no time to lose. He asked Philippe to go with him to see the Martial family. 'They were great people. Cool and very attentive to Anthony and his future. Both his parents and brothers were extremely kind and friendly. We met in Paris. I presented our career plan, from age thirteen to fifteen and from fifteen to eighteen, with a final evaluation and a series of objectives to be reached, both in terms of football and schooling. I explained that the boy would live at a boarding school at first and then at the training centre until he was eighteen. We took on all the living expenses, accommodation, schooling, trips to Paris and visits by his parents so they could come at least twice a month. We agreed and we quickly decided to offer them a non-solicitation contract that would tie him to the club, an official document that would go to us, the Ligue de Football Professionnel and the family. For three seasons, it prevented the player from signing a contract with anyone else and forbade other clubs from making approaches of any kind to the player.'

After this explanation is delivered by Bonneau, he adds, sarcastically: 'The English couldn't accept that he had signed with us. They were disappointed. They could have paid much more than the €30,000 we paid the family on signing the contract, and the financial plan would certainly have been more considerable, but the Martials understood that the financial side, if he trained properly, would come later. And they listened to us.'

Once the agreement had been signed, all that remained was for Anthony to move to OL. He would be thirteen in the December and he could already have moved to Lyon. 'But his mother wasn't keen. He was still too young to leave home so they decided to leave him at Les Ulis until the autumn of 2009. The only thing we asked was that he train four times a week, three with his own age category and one with the category above. And that he took part in the Tournoi 13 Ans Élite at FC Mougins and the Tournoi du Camp des Loges in Paris.'

The first tournament was held over the Easter weekend in 2009. The OL coach was Jean-Baptiste Grégoire, who remembers the new Paris purchase well: 'He lacked training and fitness. He couldn't keep repeating his exertions or notch up game after game at a high-level event. More than anything he played on his natural qualities, his speed and instinct. He had something others didn't but he didn't know how to get the best out of himself. In fact, he didn't score at all. But I was still disappointed I didn't get to use him in the final. It was played at six in the evening, when Martial, as well as two other members of the team from Paris, Louis Nganioni and Zakarie Labidi, had to catch the train home. We had to take to the pitch without them and we lost 1-0 to Montpellier.'

At the Tournoi du Camp des Loges, from 30 May to 1 June 2009, on paper the assessment of Anthony was not a positive one: three assists but no goals to his name. His coach's opinion was more forgiving: he recognised his considerable attacking potential, dribbling ability and ball skills, but, once again, he lacked foundations. One thing was clear … when he arrived in Lyon he would have to work, work and work some more if he wanted to break through.

Chapter 5

Discovering a new world

The Plaine des Jeux de Gerland is teeming with people on a late-September weekend. This is where the Olympique Lyonnais Academy teams come every Saturday and Sunday to play their home matches. One after the other, boys and girls of all ages in their white strip throng the plane-tree-lined aisles that lead to the many synthetic and grass pitches. Their parents are never far away. Particularly the fathers. Along the handrail or behind the fence, ready to comment on the performance of their prodigal son or daughter. Some have even brought their own folding chairs for a little extra comfort.

The OL Under-15 team is currently in the dressing room. At the end of a long corridor lined with insignia in the colours of the city's clubs, you can just make out the noise of studs on the ground, the squeaking of a sports bag zip and the voice of the coach, Joël Fréchet. He is talking them through the team sheet he has just posted on a large piece of white paper on the wall: 'Kévin and Marwan on the wings. Farès up front, supporting Berthier.' What about Anthony Martial? On the bench!

It had been the same story since the start of the season. Anthony had often been substituted and this time he had not even been picked to start the game. It was a long way from a dream start in his new team colours. The boy who thought he was going to lay waste to everyone and rack up goals as he had done back at home near Paris was biding his time champing at the bit alongside the other substitutes.

Since arriving in Lyon Anthony had been discovering the day-to-day life of an apprentice footballer. His brother Johan had almost certainly warned him about it, but he had not expected it to take him such a long time to get going. 'His first months at the club were quite difficult,' remembers Fréchet, who has since become the coach of the Under-19 team. 'He was surprised to begin with, but it's normal for there to be an adjustment phase when a boy makes a change in his life, leaves his family to live at a boarding school and discovers the demands of a professional club, both on a sporting as well as an educational level.' It was a slow period of adjustment but a logical one as far as Jean-Baptiste Grégoire, who managed the training sessions for fourteen-year-old strikers back then, was concerned: 'We tend to want to go too fast and forget that these kids have been uprooted. There are so many changes for them all at once, and to some extent that was also why we got Anthony to come a year early. To give him time to adapt, without any pressure, so that he would be in the best possible place when he moved up to the training centre. We had to push him a bit because he wasn't used to making an effort but he was always happy to be on the pitch. Playing football every day was great as far as he was concerned.'

Since the start of the 2009–10 academic year, the boy who was once a star at Les Ulis spent his weeks staying at the Collège Saint-Louis-Saint-Bruno boarding school on Rue des Chartreux in the first *arrondissement*. Here the children on the OL sports study programme rub shoulders with budding basketball players from ASVEL Basket, as well as athletes from other disciplines such as rowing and tennis. Despite his reserved character, Anthony quickly made friends among his new teammates and formed a close bond with a defender, Pierre Ertel, whom he met during his tournament trials with OL. With his help, Anthony soon discovered the rhythm enforced on those in the sports study programme, with five training sessions per week in addition to the standard academic curriculum for pupils in Year 10. Pierre Ertel recalls: 'He was shy at first but once we got to know each other we became very close. It's true that it was hard for him to start with. His head was in the clouds. He was often late and sometimes so tired he would fall asleep in class.'

Anthony Martial's typical day did indeed resemble an obstacle course for a young player described back then as 'lethargic', 'cool' or 'too quiet'. He would wake up at 7 am for a compulsory breakfast. School lessons would start at 8 am and finish at 3 pm, when he would go straight to Plaine des Jeux de Gerland by bus and run to the dressing room. Training would last from 3.30 pm to 5 pm, when he would shower and be shuttled back to the residence. Homework in the study hall would follow, then dinner and finally some free time before lights out at 10 pm. It would start all over again the next day. 'When you come from Paris to such a strict boarding school, it's obviously not going to be easy,' recognises Joël Fréchet. 'That's why he didn't play much in the first few months. I was waiting for him to finish adapting and then click into it.'

Anthony needed to make his mark in his new team, especially since he was the only rookie to join the Olympique Lyonnais Under-15 team that year. He had to blend into a group that knew everything there was to know about each other after several seasons playing together. A team that included a solid defender Romaric N'Gouma and Farès Bahlouli, who was outstanding on the ball. They were a generation of players born in 1995 who promised a bright future and were already being compared to the 1991 generation (Alexandre Lacazette, Clément Grenier and Yannis Tafer) and even the golden generation of 1987, with its stars Loïc Rémy, Hatem Ben Arfa and Karim Benzema. The 1995 generation slowly got to know the 'Parisian.' 'It was difficult at first,' explains one of Anthony's best friends from training, Romaric N'Gouma. 'He didn't open up much to people. We thought he was stern and a bit mysterious, that he only cared about himself and wasn't bothered about anyone else. But that wasn't how it was at all. He was just quiet and reserved. It didn't go all that well on the pitch either. He trained how he wanted to half the time, so he wasn't playing much at all. But one day he started working and opened up to everyone else.'

This may well have been the famous 'click' his coach was waiting for, ready to launch him into the deep end once and for all. Although Fréchet was still somewhat reluctant to make him a fully-fledged first team player, he claims he was immediately aware of Anthony's potential: 'We knew he had pure talent and that he was a kid with above average, if not extraordinary gifts. We knew he was going to climb the ladder. He was better than the others, although there was still plenty of work to be done.'

The difficult time Anthony had adjusting concerned those around him for a while. At home they had not yet given in to panic but initial questions began to arise and the first signs of impatience could be felt. His parents went to Lyon every weekend and instead of staying at Saint-Bruno, Anthony would go with them to the hotel. Florent and Myriam realised he was spending more time warming the substitutes' bench than playing. But they refrained from making waves. An instructor at the club notes: 'One of the keys to his success was undoubtedly his stable family environment. They encouraged him but never put any pressure on him. Nor did his agent, who looked after and protected him.'

True to his character, Anthony did not let anything show. He was biding his time. It finally came during a Wednesday afternoon match at the Plaine des Jeux de Gerland. His agent Philippe Lamboley was in attendance after accompanying another player to OL for a trial. Watching from the touchline, he was quickly reassured by the performance of his protégé: Anthony was having a fantastic day. He scored three goals in 80 minutes. After the match, Lamboley caught his TGV train back to Paris and went to reassure the Martial family. Anthony was gradually finding his feet in Lyon and his adaptation was on the right tracks.

The three goals he scored in the training match helped him in more ways than one. As well as reassuring those around him, they also won him a place in the starting eleven for a league game the following Saturday. Not being one to pass up an opportunity, he scored another three goals, drawing admiration from his teammates: 'We worked out quickly that he was one hell of a player,' confirmed Pierre Ertel. Anthony was even on the receiving end of congratulations from his coach: 'The players have to make an effort but the coaches also have to give them the confidence to make sure it continues to happen, and that's how it worked with Anthony. You have to get to know him, talk to him, win his trust. You have to dig down deep to discover an interesting, rich and jovial person. He may not be the most expansive person in the world but he's charming.'

The defenders who crossed his path in the Championnat Fédéral 14 Ans would likely not have used the word 'charming' to describe him … they would probably have called him a nightmare! After three difficult months, Anthony scored goal after goal. He was a little bigger and more solid than the others and despite his still somewhat lethargic side, he was already capable of reeling in defenders before spinning around them and scoring. His technical relationship with Farès Bahlouli was hard to believe. It looked as if the two kids had been playing together for years. As Fréchet recalls simply: 'Good players quickly find each other on the pitch.' They passed the ball backwards and forwards from one to the other, without forgetting their teammates. They would take it in turns to score and congratulate each other. Anthony was now nicknamed 'Toto' by the dressing room. He had been fully accepted by the group. His coach was constantly pushing him to do more and more, to score again and again. During a tournament in Bastia, Fréchet grabbed Anthony by the shirt before he went onto the pitch. He told him: 'You'd better score two goals!' ... and he scored two goals. 'It's true that there was this constant challenge between us. I always asked more from him,' confirms the coach, who was in charge of Anthony when he was fourteen. 'I did it because I knew he was capable. He had the mentality to go very far indeed.'

Anthony also showed his potential representing the Rhône-Alpes region at the Coupe Nationale for Under 15s. It was played every year on the pitches at Clairefontaine, where he had been turned down two years earlier. He began quite timidly: 'He was still a bit puny and in the first two matches he started as a substitute and didn't get much time on the ball,' a spectator remembers. But in the third match, played on the 'Pierre Pibarot' pitch at the Centre Technique National, he impressed the crowd: 'The Rhône-Alpes squad was playing Île-de-France, who hadn't lost a match since the start of the competition, and in front of all the technicians from the federation, he stood out. He scored two or three goals and his team won 3-0. Matches like that are the sign of a great future.'

News of this performance reached his instructors and teammates in Lyon. It was much talked about and helped make Anthony one of the leading lights of the 1995 generation. When it came down to the end of season interview, which determined whether the fourteen-year-old players would progress through the doors of the training centre, the 'Martial case' was decided immediately. 'He passed with flying colours. He had the statistics, as well as everything else he needed to succeed,' confirms Fréchet. 'He took a little bit longer to adapt but what did those three months matter in all the years he spent at OL? He never gave up and he worked hard. We love having kids like him.' He was not bad as a teammate either. By now Anthony had fallen in with the rhythm of life at the boarding school. His free time often came down to improvised football parties in the school playground with a bench as a makeshift goal. Pierre Ertel has not forgotten how much cheek he could show their uncompromising supervisor, Monsieur Martin though: 'When he asked us to give him our mobile phones before we went to bed, Anthony had come up with a trick and gave him his MP3 player instead. And it worked. He was great!'

Chapter 6

Already at national level

'Faster, Anthony! You're on in five minutes.' The voice of Jean-Claude Giuntini reaches Martial's ears like a clarion call. Far from appearing troubled or surprised, the Lyon striker shifts up a gear. Behind the goal, he applies himself to repeating the warm-up movements that have been drummed into him from a young age in order to get his body ready for action and avoid injury: windmills with his arms, quad stretches, bursts of speed, side shuffles … Anthony is calm, impassive and concentrated, but in just a few minutes, he'll be making his debut for the France Under 16 team.

It was all change for him at the start of the 2010–11 season. Firstly, he had to move from the Collège Saint-Louis-Saint-Bruno boarding school, just above Lyon, to the training centre, right in the heart of the Centre Tola-Vologe in the south of the city. From his new bedroom, Anthony had an uninterrupted view of the three grass training pitches used only by the professionals. He had a front row seat to watch the precision drills carried out in front of goal by the Argentine Lisandro López and the French internationals Bafétimbi Gomis and Jimmy Briand. This time Anthony quickly found his feet in the modern building with about twenty beds, especially as he had been joined at the club by two other 'Parisians', who had undergone a trial at OL alongside him two years earlier. They were the defender

Louis Nganioni (FC Bretigny) and the left winger Zakarie Labidi, who spent time at AC Boulogne-Billancourt and the INF Clairefontaine. 'He had arrived in Lyon a year before me,' remembers Labidi, who has since signed with OL as a professional. 'His bedroom was at the end of the corridor and we didn't see him much because he loved sleeping. He was big on sleeping! We would often watch TV series or films at the centre, and listen to music. He loved Sinik, the rapper from Les Ulis, and the PlayStation of course.'

Anthony loved football more than anything, particularly when it came to the console: 'He would often take PSG or Bayern Munich,' remembers a former resident of the centre. 'But he still preferred showing what he was capable of on the pitch.' This he was able to do as soon as he arrived at the training centre, particularly during an early season match against his own 1995 generation and older players born in 1994: 'It was the first match of the year,' remembers Mour Paye, also a striker but one year older than Anthony. 'Before the match, we'd already heard about him but hadn't seen what he could do yet. He brought us nothing but misery. He already had great technique. He was strong and very skilful in front of goal. We lost either 4-1 or 5-1 and he scored four goals!'

Anthony won the respect of his elders and, in passing, impressed Stéphane Roche, a former OL professional who had returned to the club that year to train the national-level Under-17 team: 'I came from Caen with a fresh eye and a group did quickly break away to compete for the France Under-17 championship. I decided to include some first year players with the 1994 generation and Anthony was one of those. I noticed him immediately. He had unusual qualities: a rhythm that was already matched by his technical skill in the box, something that is very rare in such a young player.'

As a result, Anthony skipped the Under-16 level and was immediately moved up to play with the 1994 generation. In early September, aged just fifteen and a half, he discovered the Under-17 championship during a clash against AJ Auxerre. At the end of the summer of 2010, he had another surprise: a few days later he was called up for his first official match with the France Under-16 team. He was picked for two friendly matches against Belgium alongside three other Lyonnais players, Romaric N'Gouma and his two fellow 'Parisians', Labidi and Nganioni.

Tuesday 21 September 2010 at Clairefontaine was to end in disappointment, however. Anthony was the only one of the four OL players to start the match on the bench. He had been overlooked in favour of the Caen striker Daniel Brunard. 'It's important to remember that his birthday falls at the end of the year,' remembers his first coach, Jean-Claude Giuntini. 'With players like him you had to be demanding, but give them time to grow as well.' But the former Les Ulis player had no time to lose. As soon as his coach gave him the nod, he sped off to go through his warm-up, removed his tracksuit and checked his laces one last time. In the 62nd minute, he came on for Brunard to spearhead the attack for the 'Bleuets'. The score was still 0-0. Martial had made up his mind to show Giuntini what he was capable of. His former coach remembers what happened next: 'He had barely been on the pitch for two minutes when we managed to get a cross into the box. I saw Anthony jump, win his duel with the Belgian defender, and head the ball down. It wasn't a particularly powerful shot but it was in the right place. It was his first goal for the team.'

For the record, France beat Belgium 3-0 and Anthony

was also responsible for an assist that led to France's second goal. It was what is known as scoring points …

Anthony seemed fully committed during his second season at OL. His time was split between school work – after Year 10, he began working towards a vocational certificate in heating engineering – and the pursuit of his apprenticeship as a footballer, in the shirts of both the French national team and Olympique Lyonnais. Although the talent and potential were there, there was still plenty of work to do: 'Anthony was still young in his approach to the profession and the high standards you need to have to get to a very high level,' remembers Stéphane Roche. 'He had to learn how to train better. He tended to be selective with his drills. He needed to be very exacting and push himself, particularly to learn to remain focused until the very end of a match or training session.' The OL Under-17 coach was keeping his star generation 1995 striker under wraps. He used him sparingly, especially because he also had another striker in his squad on which the club had staked a great deal. Yassine Benzia had joined OL at the start of the season from US Quevilly. He arrived with a big reputation and the status of top striker for the France Under-17 team. It was difficult for Anthony to compete with him at first: 'I wanted him to carve out a niche for himself,' explains Roche. 'Although he had joined our group at the start of the season, I wanted him to get involved in the matches gradually, so that he would also learn to be a substitute and to be patient.'

His stand-by status and the presence of Benzia did not seem to concern Anthony, however. Just as he had done for the national team, he seized his chance on several occasions and twice scored two goals during the first six league matches. 'Anthony had great confidence in himself,' Gérard Bonneau sums up. 'He didn't see his rivals as competition but rather as another challenge to be overcome in order to progress. When he arrived in Lyon he immediately understood that he was there to take someone else's place but that there was also someone behind him wanting to take his.'

During the first part of the season, Martial was picked once again as the striker for the France team for a tournament in the Val de Marne, where he scored twice against Portugal. He then played again in two friendlies in Wales in December, just a few days after celebrating his sixteenth birthday. But it was not until January that Anthony's football began to take on an added dimension. One match in particular confirmed his rise up the ranks, the seventeenth match of the season against FC Sochaux. A crucial fixture in the race to the title of Under-17 French champions, OL were without Yassine Benzia. The absence of the Under-17 team's regular striker left the field clear for Anthony Martial.

'With Benzia, there were few opportunities for Anthony to be in the starting eleven,' confirms Romaric N'Gouma, who was also in the team that day, in central defence. 'Against Sochaux, who were just behind us in the table, it was a dream match for him to show what he could do. The coaches had put him under a lot of pressure, but he did everything he could.'

In this finely balanced match that remained even for quite some time, Anthony made the difference for OL. He turned the match around with two individual efforts in the second half. Once again, Anthony showed everyone that he knew how to stand up and be counted during important games.

Despite his tender age, he hung on and tried to keep up with the older Yassine Benzia throughout the end of the season. The two OL strikers responded to one another almost every weekend on the pitch. Benzia scored hat-tricks against

Mâcon, Grenoble and Mulhouse … Anthony scored against
Clermont, Mâcon and Pontarlier; Benzia scored twice against
Pontarlier and Montferrand … Anthony scored against
Pontarlier and Besançon. This healthy rivalry between the
two strikers allowed OL to finish the season with the best
strike force in the Under-17 French championship. But the
title of champions was not to be theirs. OL disappointed
during the final stages, played in Canet-en-Roussillon, with
defeats against Marseille and Bordeaux and a lone victory
over Sochaux (with one goal from Anthony). When it came
down to it, it was logical that Benzia would take all the
acclaim. He finished way out in front with 36 goals scored
in the Under-17 league. Anthony followed with fifteen goals
in 21 matches, ahead of the other strikers from generation
1994. 'That season allowed us to test his ability to become
a leader. And although it wasn't easy in comparison with
older players such as Benzia and Corentin Tolisso, who had
more character', says Stéphane Roche, 'this reinforced our
idea about speeding up the process while allowing him to
continue his development unhindered.'

Anthony had nothing to be ashamed of after his first
season at the training centre. On the contrary, it was full
of promise. The fifteen goals he scored with OL could
be added to the nine in fifteen matches for the French
national team, and his first two trophies won with the
Bleuets at the Val de Marne (France) and Aegean Cup
(Turkey) tournaments.

'During this first year at the training centre, he showed a
real disposition for playing at the highest level,' concludes
Roche. As a reward, Anthony signed his first apprentice
contract. He earned slightly more than the base salary of
€700. Not exactly remarkable but a further gauge of confidence in his future.

Chapter 7

The new baby *gone*

Ludovic Giuly, Frédéric Kanouté, Loïc Rémy, Hatem Ben Arfa, Karim Benzema, Alex Lacazette … The list of strikers trained by OL is a long one. And almost all of them swear by Armand Garrido. He does not have years of playing professional football behind him but started out as an amateur coach for a small club in the outskirts of Lyon, AS Buers Villeurbanne. Twenty years later and he is the leading exponent of the Olympique Lyonnais style of training.

Back in the 90s, he was responsible for bringing Giuly through when no one really believed in Olympique Lyonnais because it was so small. He was also the one who brought out Karim Benzema's full potential. So what about Martial, the new baby *gone*? During the 2011–12 season, Garrido took over the reins of the Under-17 national championship team when Stéphane Roche needed to take a twelve-month break to update his qualifications. For almost a year he coached Anthony, who, alongside his friends from the 1995 generation, dreamed of being crowned league champions in their age category at the end of the season. Garrido quickly made an accurate assessment of the new jewel in the training centre's crown: 'At first glance, I discovered a boy who had all the advantages, so many advantages. He had everything he needed to succeed. Anthony is a goal-scorer but he also has a lot of pace. He has the ability to get past his opponent quickly, to string together lots of sudden and heavy strikes. He also has a good physique, a power that allows him to be strong in one-on-ones. He was quite simply born to be a centre-forward, built to be a striker. Afterwards, when I looked a bit more closely, at that time there were lots of things he needed to improve. His basics were not great and he didn't like working on that kind of thing. You had to push him. The other main problem was how he was, the fact that he was a bit dozy and you just wanted to give him a shake. It was nothing serious though, he was never fazed by anything. He was quiet at training and during matches. Sometimes he did extraordinary things and other days it was as if he had just left his calling card in the corner of the pitch.'

The experience of the season he had already spent with the Under-17 national team allowed Anthony to start off on the right foot and to be the number one offensive weapon for Olympique Lyonnais in the championship. Alongside Bahlouli, Cabon, Collet, Kalulu and of course Labidi, every weekend was a treat: one goal in the first match followed by three hat-tricks in the early autumn against Jura Sud, Grenoble and most importantly in the 4-1 derby win against AS Saint-Étienne, OL's sworn enemy. Anthony even managed the feat of scoring six goals in the same game, a 9-0 win over FC Gueugnon on 20 November. Mid-way through the season in late December, he had already scored 21 goals in ten league matches. They were exceptional statistics, but, true to his reputation, Garrido would wipe the slate clean at the start of every new week. He always expected more from his striker. He asked for more effort, more attention and more desire, and he used all his skills as an instructor to achieve this: 'There are several different ways of teaching players: first, there's discussion; there's also flattering them, when you start to get to the player a bit; and then, indifference, when you let the player do whatever they want to do. This often results in them sinking down before they recover again. With Anthony, I never found the right way to make this work. Shouting at him was useless because he would just keep doing it. Letting him get on with it was a possibility, but you couldn't always depend on him being demanding with himself. Eventually, it was discussion that worked best. You had to explain things to him and let him take his time, but you still couldn't be sure you would get the right result in the end. Although he was listening, sometimes it was as if he couldn't hear.'

The season in question was a match within the match between Anthony and his coach. Garrido did not let him get away with anything. He would mark him tightly, man-to-man like a good defender. One particular anecdote sums up their special relationship. At the Olympique Lyonnais training centre, the story is still doing the rounds of the dressing room. It goes back to 1 April 2012. That Sunday, OL were playing a late kick-off match away at Saint-Étienne on the eighteenth day of the championship season. Les Verts were keen to get their revenge after the beating they received when the two teams had met in Lyon. OL were on their guard. Departure time for Saint-Étienne had been set for 11 am. Like all the instructors, Garrido was particularly fussy about punctuality. But when they were ready to leave, he was still missing three of the sixteen players he had picked, including Anthony Martial. Garrido flew into a rage because Anthony had already been late for breakfast and despite the importance of the match, he told the bus driver to leave. In the rear view mirror, the coach saw the three latecomers come hurtling out of the training centre with their heavy bags on their shoulders and their baggy tracksuits unfastened. He ordered the driver to speed up. He had decided it was time to teach them a lesson.

'The coach really did seem prepared to do without his leading striker for one of the most important matches of the season,' recalls a member of that team. 'But I think he soon came to his senses and, after driving once around the Stade de Gerland, we were back where we started a few minutes later.' The three players, who were still by the side of the road, had been given a real fright. But that was not the end of it, particularly for Anthony. 'He wasn't the only one,' Garrido acknowledges. 'But he was a habitual offender and, as I'm sure you can imagine, I gave him a friendly reception.'

'When Anthony got on the bus, he was really angry with him,' his former teammate continues. 'He criticised him and really wounded his pride by telling him that Karim Benzema had ten Anthony Martials in each leg. That really got to him.' As a result, the boy from Les Ulis started the game on the bench. He looked on helplessly, unable to stop the Saint-Étienne domination. 1-0, 2-0 and even 3-0. After an hour of play, Garrido finally decided to bring on his striker, who had been stamping his feet impatiently on the touchline for several minutes. Anthony managed to reduce the deficit, but the damage had already been done and OL lost the derby 3-1. 'Looking back, I don't think it was a good idea because we lost the match. In the end, it wasn't a big deal. He was only a tiny bit late but I had to show him that he would be treated in the same way as all the others.'

As the months went by, Armand Garrido finally began to understand the unusual, endearing and unflappable character he was confronted with every day. 'You have to get into his world to understand his personality. He is exactly the same at training or in a match as he is normally. Cool.

He gets up like it in the morning and goes to bed like it at night. If you put a football match in the middle of it, he will try to do his best without putting himself under any pressure, and at the end of the match he returns to being the same boy that he always is ... cool, peaceful and never bothered by anything. At the beginning we thought this might hinder his progression because we struggled to understand his motivation. But, despite appearances, he's definitely much more affected than you might think. And this relaxed nature of his even helps him because he's never under pressure. Whereas some players don't sleep for three nights before a big match, he seems impervious to all that.'

Consequently, Martial was always there on the big occasions, when the pressure was at its greatest. Against AJ Auxerre, he scored the winning goal at the end of an incredible match that ended 4-3. Just after the opposing team equalised for 3-3 in the 90th minute, he committed to the ball and after a series of passes scored a cool, calm and collected goal that sent OL into the final stage of the French championship. Four days earlier, he had already made a good impression in his first match with the Under 19s. Not at all inhibited by finding himself alongside older players such as Corentin Tolisso or the Cameroonian number 1, Clinton Njie, he left his mark against AS Monaco with two goals in less than six minutes. According to Labidi, this was typical of Anthony:

'With him, nothing was impossible. He wasn't a leader in the dressing room, but on the pitch he always helped the team get the best out of themselves. This was also the case for the French Under-17 team, where he played some very high-level matches.' That year, 'Toto' also made the Bleuets happy: he scored nine goals in twelve matches for the team, including a hat-trick against Northern Ireland during qualification for the European Championships. However, his adventure with the team managed by Jean-Claude Giuntini came to an end in the first round of the Euro Under-17 finals, played in Slovenia in early May, with two poor games against Iceland and Georgia and a defeat against Germany. Anthony returned to Lyon disappointed and carrying a forearm injury. Despite this, he still had one last aim: to win the French Under-17 title with the 1995 generation. 'He had this ability to move on quickly,' explained an instructor at OL. 'Despite his broken wrist, he remained confident and told us "Don't worry, I'm going to play." He was completely in control of what he was doing. A bit like a golfer who hits a bad shot but can then refocus very quickly.'

Once again, Anthony made his appearance. With a protective cast on his wrist but on the pitch just as he had promised. Despite a long season spent switching between the OL and French teams, he still found the necessary resources to shine brightly during the final stage of the championship, which saw teams from OL, Châteauroux, OGC Nice and Paris Saint-Germain brought together in La Rochelle in Charente-Maritime. Only the winner of this mini-championship would progress to the final. It all seemed to get off to a good start for Lyon with a 2-1 victory over Châteauroux, with one goal from Anthony, followed by a poor 1-1 draw in the clash with Paris Saint-Germain. The challenge of the final game was a simple one: beat Nice and OL would qualify for the final. On 26 May 2012, Anthony was brilliant yet again. He opened the scoring in the 22nd minute by getting around the keeper. Nice then equalised. 1-1 at half time. In the 51st minute, Anthony won the advantage back for his team with a good ball from Bahlouli. 2-1. But Nice once again found the strength to come back: 2-2 just a few minutes from the end. OL were getting ready to leave the competition with their heads held high but then their final chance presented itself: Anthony won the ball with his back to goal. He was in the box, slightly off-centre to the right. He gave the ball a quick shove before spinning and passing the keeper. He kicked the ball again, this time to dummy a defender who was trying to intervene. The crowd barely had time to murmur when he unleashed a sudden shot and crossed the ball into the corner of the net. 3-2 and OL had qualified for the final. The spectators at the small Stade d'Aytré were in no doubt that Anthony Martial was a future champion. After the match, Garrido watched on helplessly as the new baby *gone* was crowned. 'There was no doubt that he had been exceptional in all three matches. He was better than everyone else. He had had some great matches and scored some super goals. By the time he left La Rochelle he had become a local star. Everyone wanted to take his photo, he was signing autographs all over the place. To be honest, I was scratching my head when we got back to Lyon, wondering how I was going to handle him with a final to prepare for.' The Lyonnais coach's fears would be justified a week later. OL were beaten 4-3 by RC Lens after being ahead on three occasions. This time Anthony was nowhere to be seen.

Chapter 8

Welcome to the pros

Forty-three goals in 36 official matches at the end of the 2009–10 season. The record speaks for itself. It was better than Karim Benzema and Alexandre Lacazette at the same age. The management at OL had to act fast as it would be difficult for them to keep their star player under wraps for much longer. Word of Anthony's performances had long since reached beyond the green rectangles of the Plaine des Jeux de Gerland. Everyone was talking about him at the club. The professional staff had got wind of the huge potential of the former Les Ulis player several months earlier, in particular, the recruitment manager, Florian Maurice, himself a star for Olympique Lyonnais in the 1990s and a French international striker who had spent time in the Spanish league with Celta Vigo: 'To be honest, I haven't seen many who were as good as he was at that age! Perhaps Cristiano Ronaldo and the other Ronaldo, the Brazilian, but that's it. Antho has Cristiano's technique but he also has an innate strength when taking the ball and making a break.' Although Florian Maurice was in the habit of searching far and wide for the next big thing, back then he believed the next star of world football could be right under his nose at the Lyon training centre.

On fan forums and social networks, the French club's supporters were having a field day: 'We've got the new Benzema', 'Can't wait to see what Martial and Lacazette will do together one day', 'With him, magnificent things are coming'. Broadly speaking, this was how all the club's fans felt. But more than this buzz around a young player aged only sixteen and a half, it was the competition from Europe's top teams that concerned the powers that be in Lyon. Martial was under close scrutiny, and it was not necessarily a recent thing: 'He was known to all the English, Italian and Spanish clubs,' concedes Gérard Bonneau. 'Since his first selection for the French Under-16 team, Pierluigi Casiraghi, scout for Inter Milan, had already been to see him. And they kept coming to OL. You should have seen the foreign clubs rushing to watch him every weekend, usually there's never anyone at our Under-17 home games. They were all there, including Juventus.'

He had let the name slip. The Bianconeri were the predators most feared by the management of the Lyon academy. In order both to protect Martial and drive away the competition, there was only one solution: get him to sign a professional contract that would prevent OL having their player stolen, as had happened to plenty of other French clubs in recent years, while also reaffirming the club's confidence in their young hope. 'In his case we went straight to a professional apprentice contract. We skipped the "training contract",' remembers Stéphane Roche, who has since become director of the training centre. 'But to be completely transparent, I'm not necessarily in favour of that because with experience you tend more to notice sources of failure than success.' But OL's position in this matter was not a strong one: 'The final stages of the French Under-17 championship had been and gone and English clubs, as well as one Italian club, from just over the Alps [he laughs], were very interested.' So we decided to negotiate with his agent and it went pretty well. There wasn't even the slightest attempt at one-upmanship or a desire on the part of the player, his parents or his agent to take advantage of the big clubs in order to play games with us.'

The discussions were not dragged out and ended in a three-year professional contract. Anthony had no wish to leave Olympique Lyonnais and those around him felt the same way. Meanwhile OL clearly had no interest in letting their future star slip through their fingers.

'We gave him a salary that was slightly above the charter for a first professional contract in Ligue 1. In other words it was above the €3,000 recommended for a young player,' confirms Stéphane Roche. 'But we added bonuses to his salary that would be triggered if he became part of the professional squad with sums that would rise if he played in a match or scored a goal. That seemed important to us because at that time he was not yet a member of the professional squad. Suddenly, his remuneration actually depended on his performance.'

It is 22 August 2010 in Lyon, they are all seated quietly in the huge office belonging to the club chairman Jean-Michel Aulas. The Olympique Lyonnais boss is enjoying the last few days of his holiday in Saint-Tropez and sends his apologies. He is represented by Stéphane Roche, Florian Maurice and the finance director, Vincent Ponsot. The Martial clan is almost complete. Anthony is flanked to his right by Florent, and to his left by Myriam and his agent, Philippe Lamboley. Only his two brothers are missing. The atmosphere is friendly and relaxed, not over-the-top or fake in any way. It is straightforward, just like the family. Nevertheless, a camera sits on the end of the table to immortalise the event when the time comes. Anthony, wearing a simple white t-shirt on this warm summer's afternoon, resolutely initials and signs the multiple copies of the contract. He is undaunted, just as he is on the pitch, although he throws an affectionate or amused glance at his parents every now and then. He does not seem at ease in this large office. His still hesitant signature is a reminder that he is still a young teenager. A photographer and a cameraman from the club's official TV channel are also in the room. Anthony knows he is going to have to grant *OLTV* his first interview. Not something he revels in. With a tight jaw and a fixed but accommodating face, he looks into the camera, with a huge poster announcing the construction of OL's big new stadium in the background. His first professional interview lasts just two minutes flat:

Journalist: Signing a professional contract must be a great moment for you?

AM: 'Yes. I'm very proud to be signing my first contract and I hope everything will continue to go well and that good things will happen.'

Journalist: 'What does this contract represent?'

AM: 'We are all proud about it, my family, everyone, and I hope it all goes well …'

Journalist: 'How do you see your future now?'

AM: 'I hope I can establish myself in the reserve team and play in some professional games.'

Journalist: 'Is this a dream come true?'

AM: 'Football is everything to me. Since I was very young, I've always hoped it would come true.'

Journalist: 'How do you feel about signing this three-year contract?'

AM: 'It proves that the directors have faith in me, and I hope they will give me a chance and that everything will be fine.'

Journalist: The coach, Rémi Garde, has already

launched the career of your friend Yassine Benzia. Has that given you ideas?

AM: 'It proves that they have a lot of confidence in young players and I hope I can do what Yassine has done and pay back this trust.'

Journalist: 'It's your turn to sign a contract now after your brother, Johan, at Bastia. Is it becoming a family habit?'

AM: It's not a habit [he smiles] … but our parents are delighted about it. I spoke to my brother on the phone and he's really happy for me.'

Anthony responds immediately as the questions are fired at him. He keeps his answers short. The boy is not very talkative and returns to his spot without saying a word, almost as if he is bothered by all the attention. He is obviously intimidated, all the more so because his father is listening attentively to all his answers from just a few feet away. Florent Martial also agrees to talk to the club's official TV channel about Anthony's first professional contract. Of average build, he has a small goatee and greying hair. He immediately comes across well, speaking in a soft voice.

Journalist: 'It must be a big day for all the family?'

Florent Martial: 'It is a big day for us and we're proud that we now have two professionals in the family. It's really something.'

Journalist: 'Anthony made a difficult choice leaving Paris to come to Lyon but that choice has now paid off …'

FM: 'Yes, it wasn't an easy choice but it's proved to be the right one for him today. He has always been a

Lyonnais at heart and he's decided to stay here by signing for Lyon as a professional.'

Journalist: 'What are his strengths and weaknesses?'

FM: 'He has weaknesses, like everyone does. I think his strengths are that he's a confident child and I think that with everything he's capable of, he might get there and that's the best I could wish for.'

Journalist: 'How have you managed to have two sons who are professional footballers?'

FM: 'They get it from their father [he smiles]. But seriously, I think both of them have worked hard for it. In their minds, they wanted to be professional footballers at all costs and their success has been the result of hard work.'

Florent Martial is not much chattier than his son but his answers are sincere and there is a hint of emotion in his voice. He understands that the baby of the family has just entered a whole new world.

The time has come to bring an end to the happy interlude, which will be immortalised with a souvenir photograph of the assembled company. When the moment arrives to leave, the handshakes are warm and the shared words of encouragement sincere: 'Welcome to the pros, Anthony.'

Chapter 9

5 million euros

Two months after signing his first professional contract, Anthony took another step forward. He skipped the Under-19 category, making his debut for the Olympique Lyonnais reserve team. It was with this team that Anthony discovered senior football during weekend matches against 'dads', as the players from the training centre liked to call them. His size, speed and great confidence helped him adapt to playing against adults. 'The signing of his first professional contract didn't trouble him,' concedes Stéphane Roche, coach of the OL reserve team back then. 'It didn't lead to any impatience or frustration. Perhaps because he's a really humble person who keeps his ego for the pitch.'

Anthony quickly began to perform in the CFA [the Championnat de France Amateur, the French fourth division]. He scored for the first time against Béziers in injury time on 16 September. This gave way to a brace against Bayonne, Martigues and ... Monaco. During a late kick-off on the fifth day of the championship played on 29 September at La Turbie, at the Monegasque club's training centre, the prodigy of the Lyon attack made a big impression in OL's 2-1 win. Anthony scored the winning goal in the 74th minute; he picked up the ball almost in the middle of the pitch, before bypassing defenders and unleashing a left-footed cross from about twenty metres out that was tucked away beneath the crossbar. It was a skilful goal that may well have impressed the directors of AS Monaco.

They were also talking about Anthony in the corridors of the Lyon training centre. His professional status and performances for OL and the French youth team contributed to his popularity. Anthony was now a benchmark for the younger players who had joined the Olympique Lyonnais Academy. He had become a role model but he did not play up to it. 'He led a quiet life and didn't show off,' confirms Mathieu Boyer, project manager at the club and education assistant from 2009 to 2013. 'He was even a go-between for me with the players. Whenever I had a message to pass on, I knew I could count on him.' That season, Anthony, who had left formal education at sixteen after the first year of his professional qualification, was taking part in a class project on careers in football. Several times a week he would study subjects such as management, French, history or English. He even took advantage of this period to acquire his level one certificate in football coaching. 'In class he was one of those who participated the most,' remembers Mathieu Boyer. 'He was very pleasant, although he always had this nonchalant air that made you feel as if you'd woken him up every time you spoke to him.'

In fact, Anthony impressed his teachers as much as he annoyed them. When he began training with the professional squad, he kept this detached attitude that would sometimes irritate others when they were talking to him: 'I bumped into him one morning, when he wasn't quite awake, walking between the training centre and the dressing rooms,' recalls Robert Valette, who has spent more than twenty years coaching at the training centre. 'It was 9.30 in the morning and it was one of his first training sessions with the professionals. He was dragging his feet as he walked. I told him that if I was his coach and I saw him walking like that, he wouldn't be anywhere near my pitch. He was calm. "Keep cool, don't be nervous," as they say nowadays.'

Yet, the big day came. The announcement of his first call-up to the professional squad fell on the day of his seventeenth birthday: 5 December 2012. Anthony was one of the list of nineteen players selected to play the Israeli team from Kiryat Shmona the following day in OL's sixth match in the Europa League. The match did not count for anything because OL were already assured of qualification for the knockout stage. As a result, the coach Rémi Garde had decided to rest his first-choice players in order to throw several players from the training centre in at the deep end. Almost all of them were there: Jérémy Frick, the goalkeeper, the defenders Mehdi Zeffane and Naby Sarr, the three-pronged attack of Pléa, Novillo and Benzia, and the three young players from the 1995 generation, Labidi, Bahlouli and Anthony Martial. 'Anthony could even have made his debut a bit earlier,' claims a source at the club. 'A month earlier, in November, there was a series of injuries up front, which meant Rémi Garde had to dip into the reserves. But at the point at which Anthony was about to be called up, he too injured his knee and in the end it was the Cameroonian Clinton Njie who joined the professional squad.'

It was only a matter of time. On 6 December 2012 Anthony Martial made his official professional debut. He did not know it yet but it was also to take place beneath the gaze of one of his idols, Zinedine Zidane, who decided to attend the match while in Lyon. Anthony started the game on the bench. Alongside his friend Labidi, he had a ringside seat for the first Lyonnais goal scored by the young defender Naby Sarr in the fifteenth minute. It looked like a school playground on the bench. They were congratulating each other, shouting and hugging, before obediently returning to their seats in the Lyonnais kindergarten, where they kept warm under blankets. Another goal came in the 58th minute, this time courtesy of Yassine Benzia. With the score at 2-0, OL were safe and sound in the face of the struggling Kyriat Shmona team and Rémi Garde began to hand out the rewards. Sidy Koné came on in the 46th minute, Harry Novillo in the 70th minute and Anthony Martial in the 80th minute.

Anthony replaced Yassine Benzia. With the number 50 on his back, he came hurtling into the world of professional football. He was seventeen and one day. He did not seem overwhelmed. He was not even bothered by the large white strapping around his knee. The crowd at the Stade de Gerland treated him to an ovation … and fifteen seconds later he came close to repaying the supporters' affections.

In the press box, the *OLTV* commentator was fit to burst with excitement: 'Martial, with such a young face, is about to become one of the youngest ever Lyonnais players to taste the world of professional football. We wish him a great career, which already looks to be very promising. He's been given a big chance here and, look out, here he is with his first touch.'

Anthony was on the receiving end of a looping ball about 40 metres from the Israeli goal. With the outside of his left foot, he immediately laid it off for Michel Bastos. The Brazilian, who was much more experienced, anticipated the young player's movement and, with one touch, gave the ball back to him in the penalty area.

The excitement mounted in the *OLTV* commentary box: 'Martial asks for the ball back … perhaps for his first strike.

Yes, he sidesteps and takes a shot ... Ah, he should have hit it with his left foot.'

It was not far from being sensational. But his strike from five metres out was obviously lacking the power to beat the Shmona keeper. Never mind. Once again, it was just a matter of time. He returned to the fray. Some minutes later and he was back. This time he picked up a ball along the left touchline. With a clever sidestep, he moved back into the middle of the pitch and rounded one defender followed by another ... but his pass was not picked up. Shame. Zidane, in the grandstand, had enjoyed it anyway. Although Anthony had failed to score, he had made a big impression. On the post-match *OLTV* set, the channel's consultant, Maxence Flachez (a former OL player in the 1990s) was won over: 'There was one player who surprised me and that was Anthony Martial. When he came on he won all his one-to-ones. I haven't seen him play that much with the youth team but he has a great future. This first taste should make him want to start playing with the professionals again soon.'

He would be back as soon as he had registered a few new exploits with the Olympique Lyonnais youth teams. Particularly in the Coupe Gambardella – the French Under-19 cup – in which he stood out in all of his appearances. It looked as if he was playing against kids: he scored the winning goal in the first match of the competition against the team from nearby AS Saint-Priest (1-2); he then scored two in the following South of France round in Perpignan (0-4); and finally the equaliser for 2-2 in the last second against Bordeaux in an incredible match eventually lost by OL 9-10 on penalties.

Anthony re-joined the professionals in February 2013, this time in a Ligue 1 game that ended in a 3-1 defeat to AC Ajaccio in Corsica. He only came on for a few minutes but distinguished himself with a shot and a handful of exchanges. He was called up another seven times before the end of the championship, but he only played in two more matches: on 19 April in Montpellier, in which he was involved in Clément Grenier's winning goal at the end of the match, and on 12 May 2013 during a show-piece match against Paris Saint-Germain at the Stade de Gerland. During the few minutes he spent on the pitch, he crossed paths with the former Manchester United idol, David Beckham. OL lost 1-0 to the Parisians, who guaranteed themselves the title of French champions that night; like all the Lyonnais players, Anthony was powerless in the face of the first flush of Qatari investment in the Paris team.

At the end of the 2012–13 season, Anthony Martial ended with three Ligue 1 appearances and a Europa League match to his name. A total of 57 minutes of play and one regret: not being able to open his account of professional goals. He had scored well in other competitions nevertheless: three goals in three matches in the Under-19 championship; four goals in three matches in the Coupe Gambardella; five goals in eleven matches in the CFA; and four goals in four matches for the French Under-18 team. As far as the Martial family were concerned, there was no need to succumb to panic, his role with the professional squad would take shape the following 2013–14 season. There was no doubt about it. But on 30 June 2013, shortly after midday, an article appeared on the official Olympique Lyonnais website entitled solemnly 'Club Announcement.' One click and fans would be astonished by the unequivocal news: 'The club has today finalised the transfer of Anthony Martial to AS Monaco for the sum of €5 million.'

Chapter 10

Regrets

Anthony Martial's transfer did not come out of the blue for everyone. The day before the official announcement, a newsflash posted on the *France Football* website alerted Olympique Lyonnais' most loyal fans to the development. According to a well-informed journalist for the weekly magazine, the young Lyon player had taken a train to Monaco on 29 June 2013 and would be moving to the club in the principality once he had passed the usual medical. The rumour quickly spread around social media and in the hours that followed a group of Lyonnais supporters set up an online petition addressed to Jean-Michel Aulas. It was entitled #PetitionPourMartial. Preceded by a long text explaining why the player should stay at OL, it ended with this moving conclusion: 'Our OL is Lopes. Our OL is Gonalons, it's Umtiti, it's Bahlouli, it's Lacazette, it's Labidi, it's N'Gouma, it's Benzia and we want it to be Martial, because if he leaves, we will have lost a piece of our OL and we will feel betrayed.

'The idea of Martial leaving shocked us,' remembers Franck, who posted the petition on the www.avaaz.org website. 'The rumours of Martial possibly signing for Monaco had just reached us and we thought it was a really bad idea. From a footballing point of view because he was our biggest talent, along with Bahlouli [who was eventually also sold to Monaco in 2015], and because he had already shown some really interesting stuff on the few occasions he had played for the professional team. Back then, Martial was already better, compared to Gomis. When it came to the financial side of things, it was reasonable to think we could have sold him for more once he had exploded for us. And the third point was more "cultural". The club and Aulas were constantly rehashing the importance of the training centre and giving young players a chance. The club's biggest talent leaving the club was totally against the Lyon ideology.'

The petition quickly collected almost 1,500 signatures. It reflected the malaise that had settled among the fans who felt cheated and deprived of their most beautiful plaything: 'Sure, we didn't take it well,' confirms Olivier, one of the contributors to the 'Gone Académie' Twitter account. 'So, we decided to circulate the petition to try to reverse the situation, not least because they were selling this incredible talent for as little as €5 million.'

In the official press release that accompanied the confirmation of Anthony Martial's transfer to Monaco, the French club did not hide its motivations. They were financial, first and foremost.

'Olympique Lyonnais realised that they had to complete another transfer before the end of the 2012–13 financial year in order to comply with their financial strategy. Because they had been unable to finalise the transfer of one of the players already ear-marked for departure, including Bafétimbi Gomis, they welcomed Monaco's request for Anthony Martial, in whom they had already shown an interest several weeks earlier.'

If the club's official spokesperson is to be believed, OL tried everything to avoid having to part with Anthony Martial and the management used their contacts to try to sell another of its strikers: Yassine Benzia and Jimmy Briand were offered to several clubs but without success. Turkish and English clubs tried to make a move on Bafétimbi Gomis but the deal kept falling through. Florian Maurice was in the middle of this puzzle: 'I can't go into detail but I can guarantee that we didn't have any choice. It was heart-breaking,' confirms the linchpin of the OL recruitment team. 'Unfortunately, clubs have to deal with an economic reality. I tried to sell plenty of other players but either they didn't want to leave or we couldn't manage to reach an agreement. If these transfers had been possible, we would have been fine and we could have balanced the books because we absolutely had to sell someone before 30 June. It was exactly at that moment that Monaco came to us and said: "We don't want any of the players you're offering us, we want that one."'

'That one' was clearly Anthony Martial. AS Monaco had been courting him for several years and he had significantly impressed ASM's technical director, Riccardo Peccini. OL had no choice but to accept the offer of €5 million. Time was at a premium so the transfer was rushed through. 'We definitely felt as if OL were reluctant about the deal. I can't say that they were particularly enthusiastic in the phone calls I received,' explains Philippe Lamboley. 'But from the point at which the directors opened the door to a transfer, they began to believe that Anthony wasn't indispensable in Lyon. So, once the two clubs had agreed on the transfer fee – although we wanted, first and foremost, for him to stay at OL – we went to Monaco to listen to their proposal: they wanted to include an emerging French player in their star team. As Anthony is very sure of himself, we decided that it could work and the transfer was completed in four days.'

'He wasn't ready to leave OL. When he came back

for the break, we told him Monaco had made an offer, that Lyon had accepted it and they were expecting us in Monaco. He arrived on the Thursday morning and by the Friday he was in Monaco,' remembers Florent Martial with a hint of sadness.

As a result, Anthony Martial would not embark on his fifth season at OL. It was with a heavy heart, given how happy he was surrounded by his 'kid brothers' at the training centre. But when he thought about it, it was hard to turn down Monaco's proposal, especially because OL had failed to give him any guarantees that he would be playing come next season. He also felt that his coach, Rémi Garde, did not have complete confidence in him, probably because, like many others, he was irritated by the boy's apparent nonchalance. 'The limited amount of time he had spent on the pitch in his first professional season may have weighed in the final balance,' suggested a director at the club. 'Lyon had a serious pile-up when it came to strikers: the Argentine Lisandro López had not yet left – he would be transferred to Qatar in early August – Bafétimbi Gomis, Jimmy Briand and Alexandre Lacazette were competing for the centre-forward position and other players emerged, such as Rachid Ghezzal, Yassine Benzia and Clinton Njie, who seemed to have a head start in Garde's eyes.' As far as Lamboley, Anthony's agent, was concerned, his future may well simply have changed direction after his first professional match against the Israeli team from Kiryat Shmona: 'If he'd scored in his first match, you can be sure he wouldn't have left Lyon so quickly. The chairman, Aulas, would undoubtedly have seen more value in him and wouldn't have given him up to Monaco like that. Football is full of stories like Anthony's, in which careers are made or unmade on details.'

But as far as the Lyonnais fans were concerned, Anthony's departure brought nothing but pain. His hasty transfer led to trouble among the club's coaches. Almost all of them learned of his transfer via the official announcement or by receiving an alert from a football website on their mobile phones. Although he was the director of the training centre, this was the case for Stéphane Roche. He found out through the press while he was on holiday with his family some 40 kilometres outside Athens: 'Sometimes that's how things happen. That's football. It's true that his departure was a setback for the development of our training programme as we felt it was going to take on another dimension the following season. Once Anthony was sold, it didn't matter whether it was five, ten, fifteen or twenty million. The frustration came only from the fact that we wouldn't see him progress in an OL shirt.'

This sentiment was shared by Gérard Bonneau. He leapt around his living room when he was informed by a last minute phone call from Rémi Garde:

'He told me: "Gérard, tomorrow we're going to find out that Martial has been transferred to Monaco. I can assure you I tried to stop the transfer but no one asked my opinion." I asked him if he'd gone mad and told him that if he let him play, he would be able to sell him for €30 million. That's how much he was worth as a striker.'

OL's strategy was also questioned in the media. In its 1 July 2013 article entitled 'Martial: have Lyon made a mistake?' the Sport.fr website entered the debate: 'The departure of Anthony Martial from Lyon to Monaco has assumed enormous significance. While the sale of a seventeen-year-old player who did not even register an hour's play in Ligue 1 last season for €5 million could well be seen as a good deal, Olympique Lyonnais have incurred the wrath of

their supporters and the incomprehension of their coach.'
One thing was certain: Rémi Garde was not prepared to
shoulder all the blame. During a press conference held
on 1 July, he publicly cleared his name: 'The chairman
explained the need to me. I had to accept this transfer for
lack of another departure. Martial was a very young player.
He had joined some of our training sessions last season.
I know him well and I would have liked to spend longer
working with him.'

This was not enough to calm public opinion: 'The day
we found out about Martial's transfer', remembers a journalist speaking at the Centre Tola-Vologe training ground,
'we were almost floored. We thought OL were getting rid
of perhaps the most talented player to have ever passed
through their training centre and were somehow selling off the future centre-forward of the French team. So,
right away, we wondered two things. The first was whether
Anthony Martial would have been thought of in the same
way if he had been born in Lyon rather than in the Paris
region. And the second was whether Jean-Michel Aulas had
fully understood the potential of his player.'

There was no question that the journalists' doubts, supporters' petition and coaches' complaints would cause
Jean-Michel Aulas, who had been chairman of Olympique
Lyonnais since 1987, to back down. Instead he would
bring everyone into line by closing the case in an interview
granted to *L'Équipe*: 'I completely understand the reaction
of the people who, without knowing the reasons behind the
transfer, have been asking how we could do it. Whether a
promising player will make it or not is often random. Can
we be certain that a player who is very good at youth level
will be as good with the professional squad? If he becomes
a great player we will get the financial return but not the

footballing return. I am the person best placed to make that decision.'

That was it. OL added a series of clauses to the €5 million that would see them receive a substantial bonus in case of a future capital gain realised by AS Monaco. But the potentially beneficial financial transaction would surely not replace the on-pitch magic. 'Of course OL protected themselves, we weren't that stupid,' summarises Robert Valette, a now retired former coach for the club. 'This is what happens when you sell a young player. But there will always be regret because Nabil Fekir emerged the following year and all those who are passionate about OL will probably always regret that they never got to see the trio of Alex Lacazette, Nabil Fekir and Anthony Martial evolve together. Perhaps one day we'll see them reunited, but it will be in a France shirt.'

Before packing his bags and bringing his time in Lyon to a close once and for all, Anthony Martial had a thought for the diehards who had tried in vain to get the management at OL to change its mind. On *Radio Monte Carlo*, the new Monaco player said: 'I was told that the fans had set up an online petition. That shows that the OL fans were really fond of me and it makes me really happy. I'd like to thank them for everything they've done and wish them luck in supporting OL. This petition was a huge thing for me as I'm only seventeen. Those people had been following me since I was really young and seeing me leave without having played much for the first team must have seemed weird to them.' Regrets were undeniable …

Chapter 11

Toto and the tsars

30 June 2013 promised to be a magnificent day on the Rock. As is often the case at that time of year, there wasn't a cloud in the sky and the sun looked kindly on the principality. The Corniche offered uninterrupted views of the blue Mediterranean. Monaco was just waking up and the first tourist coaches were arriving: Russians, Japanese, a handful of Americans and the first July holidaymakers, who had succumbed to the call of their annual break a few days early that year. Summer was just around the corner. It was in this holiday atmosphere and idyllic setting that Anthony discovered Monegasque life, and the young striker savoured his happiness. His mobile phone had been buzzing non-stop with messages of congratulations and encouragement. These came from his friends in Les Ulis, family and football buddies, as well as from Rémi Garde, the Olympique Lyonnais manager, who did not hold back from expressing his disappointment: 'If you had stayed with us, you could have really taken off this season and been the surprise of the 2014 World Cup.' Monaco's latest resident betrayed the hint of a smile on reading the message from his former coach, but his adventure in Lyon was already behind him.

His transfer was finally made official by AS Monaco later that morning with a statement on the club's website:

'The young seventeen-year-old striker from Olympique Lyonnais, Anthony Martial, joins AS Monaco FC. On Sunday morning, accompanied by Riccardo Peccini, the technical director, Anthony signed his three-year contract. Once again, the club has demonstrated that its recruitment policy is looking to next season as well as to the future.'

The announcement was paired with a photo of the two men in front of the club's logo in gold letters. The new recruit, wearing a black t-shirt and a light grey jumper, poses with a wide smile as Peccini stands to his right; he is holding the famous red and white shirt out in front of him with the tips of his fingers. The picture is accompanied by the Italian director of football's initial reaction: 'We're delighted that Anthony has joined us. He's a great hope for his generation and he's going to continue his top-flight apprenticeship with us.' Simple, effective and concluded quickly as the ASM recruitment team was at full throttle during that transfer window. Anthony Martial was only one seven-figure transfer among plenty of others. Five million euros, a record in France for a player aged under eighteen but a trifling sum for the Monegasque club that did not even go to the trouble of organising a press conference to introduce their new player. 'That's not surprising,' confirms a source close to ASM. 'This club is very unusual. It's impenetrable, like the principality! There's always been a cult of secrecy here and that increased tenfold with the arrival of the Russian shareholders. They're overprotective towards the young players and try to keep them away from the media. It should also be said that not that many people were interested in Martial in 2013. It was only the experts who knew about him. Some were even wondering what role he was going to play in this mammoth project undertaken by the directors.'

You could say that again. For a little over a month, ASM had been driving the transfer market in spectacular fashion, recruiting hand over fist to prepare an ultra-competitive team capable of rivalling Paris Saint-German for the 2013–14 season. In late May, Monaco had forked out €70 million to secure the services of the FC Porto duo of João Moutinho and James Rodríguez, then, a week later, the club president Dmitry Rybolovlev put another 43 million on the table to snatch the Colombian Radamel Falcao from Atlético Madrid. The transfer of these three attacking heavyweights was followed by the arrival of the Portuguese Ricardo Carvalho, the Brazilian Fabinho, and the French internationals Jérémy Toulalan and Éric Abidal. It is not hard to see why Martial's transfer may have gone unnoticed: 'He was lost in the crowd and he had come in through the back door,' the source continues. 'In fact, there were clearly two different ways of looking at the transfer market in Monaco: on the one side were the stars such as Falcao and James Rodríguez, and on the other, young players like Martial, Borja López and Geoffrey Kondogbia. Plenty of journalists also thought €5 million was far too much for a young player like him. Personally, I was wondering mostly about how he was going to find his niche in that squad.'

On the face of things, the welcome given to the new recruit was far from lavish or unanimous. The Martial family understood this well though, and Anthony's agent was planning to play the role of an upmarket sales rep to guarantee his protégé's after-sales service. On the day of the transfer, Philippe Lamboley granted the French website *FootMercato* a first interview. There were several messages that needed to be conveyed. Firstly, that Monaco was not a default choice:

'Anthony had the chance to go to big foreign clubs, Juventus had put forward a concrete offer. A month ago, the door was closed completely and the player wanted to stay in France anyway [...] Monaco is a big club, with big ambitions that fit with Anthony's way of thinking. It's also a club that's run by foreign managers so it's a good compromise between a foreign club and a French club.'

Lamboley also wanted to restore balance in the, at first glance, unbalanced battle with Radamel Falcao for the centre-forward position: 'There was competition at Lyon too, it's not as if he has come from a third division club. He knows about big clubs because Lyon is a big club. If you want to have a successful career you have to play at clubs where there's competition. Anthony is a pure centre-forward, even if at Lyon he occasionally played on the wing because when you're young you have to know how to play in several positions. But he's a centre-forward who scores goals and is generous with his teammates. He is planning to play for the Monaco first team and it will be up to him to demonstrate his qualities. Whether a player is seventeen or 28, whether he's earning millions or considerably less than that, the manager will pick the players who will bring the best to the team, and hearing this was music to our ears. The coach has faith in Anthony and Anthony has faith in him.' Three days later, the player himself was called upon to address the issue of competition in his first interview with the regional daily, *Nice-Matin*. Although the kid from Les Ulis confirmed that 'it's a dream playing with Falcao', he repeated almost word for word what his agent had said when the journalist asked him how the directors at Monaco had managed to convince him to sign. 'They told me that it's not age that determines who's on the pitch and who isn't. The best player in training will play. Ranieri is a great coach ...'

The problem for Toto was that he would only make a handful of appearances at training during the month of July, delaying his integration into the Monegasque squad. Although this time of year at the club was devoted to intense preparation and in-depth work as a group, during the summer of 2013 Anthony would have to bear the cost of his popularity with those at the top of the French Football Federation, forcing him to go back and forth between the principality and the France team training centre at Clairefontaine.

Despite this, his Monaco adventure began on 3 July 2013. Martial was expected in Central Italy, at Roccaporena, a small hamlet in the commune of Cascia in Umbria, where ASM had begun its summer preparation two days earlier. It was there that he met some of his new teammates: 'To start with, there were lots of young players, the stars hadn't arrived yet,' remembers the midfielder Dominique Pandor. 'Anthony turned up like he always did, without making a fuss. He already knew some of the internationals of his generation, like the defender Yarouba Cissako. He must have sung something that first night at dinner, like you have to every time you arrive in a new group, but I don't really remember it. He's so reserved and he didn't stay with us for that long anyway.' Three days all in all. There was barely even time to make his first appearance on the small pitch at the foot of the hill named after the local saint Santa Rita – smiling from ear to ear and wearing his sleeveless red strip with the number 23 already printed on his shorts – before he found out he had been given a surprise call-up for the Under-19 European Championships in Georgia from 20 July to 1 August: 'He was one of four young Under-18 players I decided to bring up a category for the Euros because I had to make up for a lack of quality in attack,' remembers the coach Francis Smerecki. 'I'd been following Anthony for a while, I had already picked his big brother. I thought his attacking qualities were fantastic. His pace down the wing could bring us the dynamism we were missing.' So Toto had to repack his suitcase. This time he was headed from Italy to Georgia, but Smerecki made sure his trip was not a wasted one. He started in five of the six matches France played in the tournament, including the final, which they lost 1-0 to Serbia. Used mostly on the wing, Anthony failed to score even once but made a good impression nevertheless. 'He was already a talent,' Francis Smerecki concluded. 'And he had everything it takes to become a real gem.'

He did not know it yet but his performances had also won over another French manager. As he was getting ready to finally return to the principality after a few days well-deserved rest, his debut on the AS Monaco training pitches at La Turbie was to be postponed yet again. This time it was the brand new manager of the France Under-21 team who had succumbed to his potential. And he was not just anybody. It was a former French international defender with plenty of silverware to his name with Bayern Munich and a semi-final at the 2006 World Cup who had called him up. Willy Sagnol, who had been at AS Monaco between 1997 and 2000, wanted to make his mark in his new role and to do so called up three of the team that had finished second in the Under-19 Euros to complete his squad for a friendly in Germany. He picked Yassine Benzia (born in 1994) and two players born in 1995, who were being promoted by two age categories, Adrien Rabiot and Anthony Martial. This was almost unheard of in the Bleuets team. Sagnol gave this explanation on the FFF website:

'I have made my choice based on technical qualities. Several young players have been called up, which does not mean they will be there every time. It depends largely on how much they play for their club.' No guarantees for Anthony but a brilliant opportunity to show what he could do. 'It was a bit special how everything happened so quickly. It was like I had grown up suddenly,' recognised Anthony Martial when the team sheet was announced. This was easy to understand: when he came on for Yassine ?enzia in the 56th minute on 13 August 2013 in Freiburg he was facing players who were almost three years older because his birthday falls in December. But this first selection for the Under-21 team, also known as Les Espoirs [the Hopefuls], came with yet more good news. This time he was playing right in the centre, in his favourite position. The match ended goalless. Now it really was time for Anthony to go back to Monaco. Although these experiences with the Under-19 and Under-21 France teams had been great opportunities, there was no time to lose now. In his absence, the ASM strikers had started scoring points with Claudio Ranieri. In August, Radamel Falcao was quick to get himself noticed by scoring his first goals in a Monaco shirt, and alongside him, Emmanuel Rivière in particular was showing what he could do with five goals scored in the new season's first four league matches.

August came to an end with Anthony Martial's official debut in a Monaco shirt. In front of a crowd of no more than a hundred, Toto played in the third match in the fourth division. Far from the bright lights of Ligue 1, AS Monaco were at home to the team from Pau that night and Anthony was only involved in one half. Before leaving the complex at La Turbie almost unnoticed, he showed his hand to the few journalists who were present: 'For now, I haven't been able to show what I can do, but I hope to now that I'm back. I was reassured to see that they didn't get any other strikers after me. If I work hard, you never know what can happen.' Anthony could not yet imagine what was waiting for him …

Chapter 12

Cloudy skies over Monaco

'Subašić, Fabinho, Raggi, Kurzawa, Abidal, Moutinho, Kondogbia, James Rodríguez, Ocampos, Carrasco, Rivière, Toulalan, Falcao …'. They were all there, except Martial. Once again Anthony's name was missing from the list of players picked by Claudio Ranieri. It was 7 November 2013, the day before a match between ASM FC and Évian Thonon Gaillard FC, the thirteenth match of the Ligue 1 season, when initial doubts began to emerge among those close to the young hopeful. Anthony had come to Monaco to carve out a niche for himself in the first team, to spend more time on the pitch and to consolidate his reputation, but he had yet to play so much as a single minute in Ligue 1 after four months of competition. All he had to console him was two appearances on the substitutes' bench in October against Saint-Étienne and FC Nantes in the league, and fifteen short minutes of play in the League Cup during the loss away at Reims on 30 October. It was a drop in the ocean in terms of his ambitions.

It was also a surprising turn of events because, despite his repeated trips back and forth with the France Under-21 team – he had played in another four matches for the Bleuets in September and October and even scored against Kazakhstan – Anthony seemed to have made his mark quickly in the Monaco dressing room. This was confirmed by several sources, as well as by Anthony's agent Philippe

Lamboley: 'It wasn't that obvious though, because in order to find his place he needed to be ambitious, but not too ambitious. The aim of going to Monaco was to learn his trade alongside players like Abidal, Toulalan, Moutinho and Falcao. Anthony's strength lies in being clever and natural enough to get himself accepted easily by his teammates.'

But his integration was eased in particular by the complete support of several players, including his fellow former Lyonnais, Jérémy Toulalan and Éric Abidal: 'We were a bit like older brothers in the dressing room, we didn't worry about him too much but we tried to give him some tips,' remembers Abidal, who was at Monaco at that time after winning numerous trophies with Barcelona. 'His situation reminded me a bit of mine when I was twenty and had to leave my little club just outside Lyon (AS Lyon-Duchère) to sign for Monaco. It was obvious that Anthony really wanted to play but he also knew that he had to show he could be patient. I kept telling him not to pay attention to the manager's choices but to be ready because sooner or later he would eventually get his chance.'

The good news was that Anthony did not get discouraged. Unlike other shooting stars that have passed through the principality, he showed a mental fortitude and a fierce desire to achieve his objectives: 'He was impressive in training. He was often the best. He would take on the older players and leave them wanting in games of four against four,' recalls one of his former partners at Monaco, Anthony De Freitas. In short, Anthony did not give up and certainly did not give in to the temptations of life on the Riviera that could have seen him go off the rails. 'When you're young and you start earning money, Monaco is a dangerous club,' confirms Fabien Pigalle, an expert on ASM at the *Monaco-Matin* newspaper. 'There's no pressure from the fans but so many temptations everywhere you look, with the casinos, fast cars, beautiful women … Some players lose their way, like the Colombian Juan Pablo Pino, who was a real diamond when he was recruited in 2007. Others like Layvin Kurzawa or Yannick Ferreira-Carrasco turned themselves around just in time. Martial never allowed himself to get distracted. He quickly understood that to be successful here he needed to go to bed early, live a healthy lifestyle and, most importantly, keep his feet on the ground.'

During his first few months in Monaco, Anthony spent most of his time in his hotel room, a suite at the Novotel, a stone's throw from the Stade Louis II, where the recruits usually stayed while looking for an apartment or villa that was to their liking. As in Lyon, his favourite activities boiled down to football matches on his games console or chatting with his friends from Les Ulis and Lyon on social media. He did not have his driving licence yet so the club provided him with a car service for getting around the principality. During the week he trained with the professional squad, while at weekends he rubbed shoulders with the club's other young hopefuls at Championnat de France Amateur (fourth division) matches as part of the team managed by Frédéric Barrilaro. The Monaco coach, who had come across Martial on several occasions when he was still at OL, quickly fell under the new recruit's spell. 'I got to know a charming young man. He was reserved but got on well with everyone. With other young professionals it would have gone to their heads and they wouldn't have been happy about playing CFA matches, but not him. He had a great mindset.'

It was under this instructor's watchful eye that Anthony first experienced things falling into place in a red and white shirt. After watching the 'pro's' poor 1-1 draw at home against Évian Thonon Gaillard in Ligue 1 from the stands, he was on the pitch the following day with the ASM reserve team for the tenth CFA league match of the season against an amateur team from Marignane. If attendance had been low at the Stade Louis II the day before, on the stroke of 6 pm that Saturday night the match pitch at La Turbie was almost deserted. There were barely fifty spectators. It was a shame that so few were there to witness Martial's career take off in his new team colours. 'He was incredible in one-on-ones throughout the entire game, and in his acceleration in the first few metres. He had a bit of Cristiano Ronaldo in him,' remembers Frédéric Barrilaro enthusiastically. Martial scored three of Monaco's four goals. A hat-trick that did not surprise his teammates, such as De Freitas: 'He didn't have to force it but he was already a level above.' His performance also drew rare admiration from the opposing team. That night Samir Kouakbi was in goal for US Marignane, a small Provençal club in the fourth division. He would never forget his role in that match against Anthony Martial: 'He only needed three shots to score three goals. They weren't fantastic goals but they were a striker's goals: he scored one from inside the area and the two others from slightly further out. What impressed me was that he was always in the right place at the right time, and that he was so mature for his age. At Marignane, we were known for being able to put pressure on young players. But him … He remained impervious to all our attempts to destabilise him, it was unheard of. He scored those three goals without saying a word, then he left. We talked about it at the club for a long time after that match … We knew we'd met a future star. Even if he put three goals past me, I'm happy I crossed his path as it's given me a tiny place in history … Somehow that match was decisive in terms of how his career developed at Monaco.'

Although, as was usual, Ranieri was not in attendance for the reserve team match, the Italian coach was swiftly made aware of the performance of his young French striker. This time he could not deny the evidence: Martial had to be given his chance with the professionals. 'It was tough for us young players with Ranieri,' admits Dominique Pandor – a striker from the 1993 generation who played alongside Martial during his two seasons at Monaco. 'He never came to watch us play and because the first team was doing pretty well, he had no need to launch his young-sters in at the deep end. However, Anthony impressed us so much in all his matches that we couldn't really understand why Ranieri had never called him up. Anthony forced his hand a bit with that hat-trick.' All the more so because five days later Toto underlined it with another goal at Toulouse against Armenia for the France Under-21 team in a quali-fying match for the European Championship. This time Ranieri was all out of excuses.

The big day came on Sunday 24 November at the Stade de la Beaujoire, where Monaco were facing FC Nantes. In the 63rd minute the score was still 0-0 when Anthony came off the bench for Radamel Falcao, who had taken a knock to the thigh. As always, it was impossible to detect any emotion on the face of the kid who was about to turn eighteen but he came hurtling onto the pitch and took up his position at the forefront of the attack. Eight min-utes later, Mounir Obbadi gave ASM the win and Anthony basked in the team's collective excitement. His moment would come a week later on Saturday 30 November against Rennes, his first start in the absence of Falcao. The fif-teenth match of the Ligue 1 season was a mid-afternoon kick-off and, for the first time in his young professional career, Anthony found the back of the net. Monaco had taken the lead in the nineteenth minute through James Rodríguez and Martial steered his team home with plenty of flair: the ball fell favourably for him in the area and his left-footed cross made its way over the line with the help of the post. Benoît Costil, the Rennes keeper, became his first victim. The joy on Anthony's face looked suspiciously like intense relief. It was shared by the entire team. His team-mates took turns to congratulate their new recruit near the corner flag with a succession of affectionate gestures that spoke volumes, like the friendly tap from the captain that night, Éric Abidal: 'With my experience I knew that in spite of his talent it would be tough for him to take his place in that team. There were so many well-known players in the squad, particularly up front. But he had the chance to score quickly. Those first few difficult months had stood him in good stead. Ranieri didn't give it to him on a platter, but made him discover how difficult life as a professional footballer can be, what the flip side is like. But Anthony did well and didn't give up. He knew how to learn from this experience.'

In the dressing room after the match, Anthony took advantage of the microphone proffered by the club's official channel, *AS Monaco TV*, to get his message across, as if his goal had not been enough: 'I was hungry tonight and I wanted to show the manager he could count on me.'

Over the coming weeks, Ranieri would have several opportunities to remember his number 23 fondly as Toto strung together a series of good performances, so much so that he almost forgot the absence of his star player, Falcao: in the sixteenth match of the season, he delivered a decisive pass to Emmanuel Rivière at Nice, then scored again at Guingamp, this time with his right foot, in his first full match on 14 December 2013. His charm offensive was up and running: Anthony now had the confidence of the entire group and was beginning to catch the eye of the media. 'He was impressive against Nice and Guingamp, the only thing he is missing now is regular appearances,' wrote Mathieu Faure in *Nice-Matin*, while his manager agreed to talk about him for the first time in the post-match press conference. Ranieri was smart and beat the critics to it, explaining at the outset why he had decided to keep Martial 'warm' for nearly five months: 'I have the experience to know when is the most appropriate time to give a player a start. Anthony has become more attentive and focused. He performs well in training and is now doing the same thing in matches.' Rumours claimed that Ranieri had underestimated Martial's talent at the time, and that he was not entirely aware of the real potential of the player who arrived from Lyon without his full agreement. This was the argument put forward quietly by some at the La Turbie training centre: 'The first four months were difficult for Anthony. If you wanted to be hypocritical, you might say that it was the period of adjustment needed by a young player, but everyone at Monaco knew why he wasn't playing: Ranieri didn't think he would be ready so quickly and that he would have to pick other players before him.'

The good news for Anthony was that Ranieri finally seemed to believe in him and was even prepared to make him one of his key players going forward: 'He can do anything: he dribbles well, he has pace, he's strong and he always fits into the team. With so many champions around him, he can learn a lot. He has the qualities to become a great player, the potential to have a fantastic career if he stays focused on what he has to do. With this consistency, he can become a regular for the France team and play at the 2014 World Cup. Why not?' Why not indeed?

However, this change in attitude from the Italian manager was not good news for those clubs hoping to take advantage of his apparent blindness, or of Anthony's initial doubts, to lure the player away during the winter transfer window. This was the case for Juventus, who were continuing to monitor Anthony closely, as well as for Olympique Lyonnais and its chairman Jean-Michel Aulas, who were hoping to be in with a chance of getting their former player back on loan. Ranieri's response to these two prestigious suitors was scathing: 'Martial is ours. We paid for him.'

But unfortunately this Martial-mania was to be quickly deflated. It came to an end on 20 December 2013, just before the Christmas break. Monaco were at home to Valenciennes for the nineteenth league match of the season at the mid-way point. Before leaving for a brief holiday, Anthony wanted to strike a final blow with his fifth consecutive start, but time was not on his side. A tackle brought his game to a premature end. The verdict came after the match: a bad sprain to the left ankle and almost a month out. He was to be stopped in his tracks.

The injury would hit him hard. An ill wind would bring him little respite until the end of the season. In the winter transfer window, Monaco bought the Bulgarian international Dimitar Berbatov, formerly of Tottenham Hotspur and Manchester United, from Fulham to fill the gap left by Martial and particularly Falcao, who had a knee injury that would keep him out for six months. As a result, between his return to the pitch in early February and the end of the league season on 18 May 2014, Anthony only played in five Ligue 1 matches (starting in only two), as well as three rounds of the Coupe de France. He failed to score in any of those games. Suffice it to say that when the time came to make an assessment (fifteen matches, two goals and one assist), his first season in Monaco left a bitter taste in his mouth. It had been a gruelling 2013–14 season that reminded him how difficult the path he had chosen could be and that he still had a long way to go before finding his feet in Ligue 1. Anthony knew more than ever that he would have to make a better show of himself if he was to chase away the clouds once and for all next season.

Chapter 13

Punishment

To understand the incredible scenes that played out on 25 August 2014 on the pitch at the Stade de Beaujoire during a French Ligue 1 match between local club FC Nantes and AS Monaco, we need to cast our minds back to something that happened just over four months earlier. We need to look back to the day before the Coupe de France semi-final, which ASM would lose after extra time against En Avant de Guingamp. To Tuesday, 15 April to be precise. That day, during the pre-match press conference, Claudio Ranieri virtually sealed his future in the principality by letting slip this short phrase: 'I don't know if I'll be the Monaco manager next season …'

He clearly knew what he was talking about … The Italian coach had already been informed as to AS Monaco's change of plans and was well aware that a victory in the Coupe de France would have no influence whatsoever on the decision taken by the club's directors. Ranieri was no longer the right man for the job as far as the Russian owner was concerned. Dmitry Rybolovlev had decided to review his strategy by switching from a policy focused on star players to recruiting cheaper young talent to allow for better financial gains. Given the history of his two years in charge at ASM, Ranieri was far from the right fit for that profile. The treatment he had inflicted throughout the season on young hopefuls such as Valère Germain, Lucas Ocampos, Yannick

Ferreira-Carrasco … and Anthony Martial had not necessarily struck a chord with his superiors. 'Behind the scenes, the directors criticised Ranieri for not giving enough pitch time to the young players,' confirms the *Nice-Matin* journalist Mathieu Faure. 'It may well be that the Martial case was one of those that led ASM's directors to think that if promoting young players was their aim, Ranieri was perhaps not the right man for the job. So his contract was not renewed at the end of the season despite the fact that he had led the club to second place in the league behind PSG, even setting a new Ligue 1 points record for Monaco in the process.'

The Martial case does indeed seem to have played a part in the looming split between the two parties. All the more so because Ranieri never thought twice about making jibes at his young protégé in public. The glowing terms used at the end of 2013 had given way, during the second half of the season, to a number of digs made by the Italian, who was tired of the French player's half-hearted attitude. The incident given the most media coverage occurred during the very same pre-match press conference against Guingamp on 15 April 2014, when, after informing journalists about his future, Claudio Ranieri mentioned the Martial case in a halting French that was full of imagery: 'Anthony is a great player, he's a great young player with a big future but he has to change … how do you say that in French? Yes, his mentality. He has to change his mentality, that's it. But lots of French players are like that. The French mentality is, one day I play well, and maybe the next day too. Isn't that right? You have to be hard every day, that's what I think about Anthony. If he changes his state of mind, he could have an incredible career, he could be one of the greatest. But if he doesn't develop, he'll just be a good Ligue 1 player and nothing more! A player who will be content to earn a certain amount of money. On the other hand, if he gives himself the means and sets important goals, he can become a champion and a first team player for any club he wants. He has the right qualities and is very good, but in football that isn't enough. You have to be very good every day in training, every time you play, every night while you're asleep. If he understands that, well …'. Ranieri ended his final sentence with a hand gesture that seemed to indicate Anthony would rise very high indeed.

The Italian manager's analysis did not surprise die-hard ASM observers, who would have had the opportunity to see the complicated relationship between master and pupil on a daily basis. Nor did it surprise anyone inside the club, including its other coaches, such as Frédéric Barrilaro, who had the opportunity to discuss what was considered the French player's 'amateur' attitude with Ranieri on several occasions: 'He found him nonchalant, he had the impression he wasn't giving his all and didn't care, and that really annoyed him. When you get to know Anthony, you realise this isn't the case, but that is the impression he can give some people.' Ranieri's media outburst was not well received by the Martial clan. The player's agent, Philippe Lamboley, completely rejected the supposed image of his player and publicly reacted the following day: 'Monsieur Claudio Ranieri is very experienced and an excellent communicator. What bothers me is his way of trying to justify Anthony's lack of playing time by blaming the famous "French mentality" and the commitment that goes with it. It is important to take on board all advice, particularly when it comes from Monsieur Ranieri. Anthony can always work harder and improve, but I find it unfair to link this to the commitment, work and patience he has demonstrated all season. I don't think it's a constructive approach.'

This running battle would not continue long between the two parties: on 20 May 2014, three days after the end of the French league season, Claudio Ranieri was given his cards as manager of AS Monaco. He was replaced immediately by the Portuguese Leonardo Jardim, who had just finished a great season in charge at Sporting Portugal and was poached for an offer of €3 million. Jardim came with the tag of someone known for nurturing young talent. The ideal manager for ASM ... and perhaps also for Anthony.

However, replacing Ranieri with Jardim was not enough to put an end to the discussion that had been taking place for several weeks now among those close to Anthony. A source close to the club reports: 'As far as they were concerned, there was no question that Anthony would stay here and vegetate for another season, so they were seriously considering whether Monaco was the ideal club to help him develop.' They seemed to be erring on the side of Anthony leaving Monaco, and this eventuality gained a foothold as the summer went on. In France, one club in particular was applying pressure when it came to securing Anthony's services: the Girondins in Bordeaux. Not necessarily the most famous team in Ligue 1 – they had finished seventh in the recent season – but a club with a strong argument to press since the arrival of their new manager, Willy Sagnol. It was Sagnol who had given Anthony his chance with the France Under-21 team almost a year earlier, and who had continued to believe in him despite the problems he was having at club level.' 'His talent was undeniable. He was in a difficult situation at Monaco and he wasn't playing,' Sagnol would later recognise for the *RTL* radio station. 'So, I tried to get him to come to Bordeaux. I sensed that he needed a vote of confidence and at Monaco he didn't seem to be getting what he needed.'

But although Anthony was obviously not immune to Sagnol's offer, Bordeaux did not have the means to meet its ambitions and could only consider bringing Martial on loan. It was difficult to tie up because if Monaco decided they did want to breathe new life into their player, they had no reason to do Bordeaux a favour, even if Sagnol was an ex-ASM man. In fact, Monaco seemed more inclined to listen to proposals from abroad. And there were many of them despite Anthony's disappointing season. Two London heavyweights, Arsenal and Tottenham, were waiting in the wings, as well as one German team, Wolfsburg, and two Spanish armadas in particular, Atlético Madrid and Valencia CF. The latter seemed the most determined and was in pole position. After failing with Jackson Martínez (FC Porto) and Álvaro Negredo (Manchester City), Valencia CF had clearly set its sights on the French player. They were said to be prepared to spend almost €15 million for the deal, allowing ASM to make a tidy profit – €10 million no less – in a single season. This gave Monaco's directors plenty of food for thought and their new manager some new cause for concern.

Since his arrival, Leonardo Jardim was facing a real exodus from his strike force as Monaco were preparing to return to the Champions League, a competition in which the club had not played for ten years. The first to leave had been Emmanuel Rivière, who signed a good contract with Newcastle United, then James Rodríguez, who took advantage of a great World Cup in Brazil, where he had finished as top scorer while playing for Colombia, to join the latest *galácticos* at Real Madrid. These two transfers finalised in mid-July had brought ASM €65 million, but now that the coffers were full, Jardim asked his directors to close the doors. Despite this, they remained open to one final pass out for Anthony Martial or … Radamel Falcao, who was also applying pressure to leave. One of the two would be able to leave if Monaco could find the right destination before 31 August 2014, while the second would stay, regardless of what happened in the principality, to assist Dimitar Berbatov and Valère Germain in attack.

And so this brings us to the famous night of 25 August 2014, to the last match of the day in the third round of fixtures for the new 2014–15 Ligue 1 season. ASM travelled to Nantes for a 9 pm kick-off broadcast at prime time on *Canal+*. It was a little after 10.20 pm when Anthony began preparing to come on. It was the 61st minute. His team had been in the lead since the end of the first half thanks to a goal from Falcao. For a second time that season – he had played fifteen minutes against Lorient in the first match of the season – Martial replaced Lucas Ocampos for the final half hour of play. Jardim gave him his final pieces of advice and Anthony agreed. He did not know it yet but he would not see the game out … at 10.48 pm, in the 88th minute of play, Jardim requested a final substitution although the score had not changed, and, in an act rarely seen, Anthony was recalled to the bench to allow Yannick Ferreira-Carrasco to finish the match. He was not even injured but here he was forced to give up his place after only 27 minutes on the pitch. Once the incomprehension had passed, thoughts quickly turned to the possibility that this change was a sanction: 'All week, instructions had been repeated in training, and Jardim had insisted heavily on always staying in the right position and coming back to defend,' according to Mathieu Faure from *Nice-Matin*. 'And as Martial failed to respect those instructions when he came onto the pitch, Jardim simply decided to take him off. It was terrible to watch. He had been humiliated live on *Canal+*. But what is fascinating about him is that when he was coming off he betrayed no emotion at all, his face was impassive. You could see that he was strong and that moment marked the starting point of his Monaco story.'

After that match, a 1-0 victory over FC Nantes, Jardim attempted to defuse the situation by claiming that substituting Martial was merely 'a tactical choice', but no one was taken in and it had been a by-the-book punishment of a player who, if truth be told, was not really in the correct frame of mind for a Ligue 1 game that evening: 'It is important to remember that we were set to leave the following day for Valencia to sign the contract,' explains his agent, Philippe Lamboley. 'The transfer was imminent. The previous week, he had not played at Bordeaux in order to avoid an injury when Jardim really wanted him to play at all costs. And against Nantes, he should never have been brought on to the pitch, he wasn't in a fit state. When he did, it ruined the start to his season ...' As it was, Anthony would never board the plane to Spain. The transfer to Valencia eventually collapsed: 'It got delayed, there was some procrastination and Falcao pushed so hard to leave that in the end Monaco kept Anthony,' Lamboley says with regret. 'It was a shame because Valencia would have been an interesting club, and with his profile, Anthony could have gone a long way in Spain.'

Radamel Falcao, who was loaned to Manchester United in the final hours of the transfer window, had been more persuasive – or shrewd – and Anthony was eventually pipped at the post. It would take him several weeks to come to terms with this two-fold insult and to throw himself back into life in Monaco. 'He had quite a few doubts,' remembers his friend and teammate, Dominique Pandor. 'But a couple of days later the manager took him to one side and spoke to him.' Jardim probably explained to Anthony that now Radamel Falcao had left, he had a clear path to step into the lead role up front for ASM. He may even have delivered the phrase that he would throw the way of the press sometime later: 'Players who spent last season hiding behind our big stars will no longer be able to do so.' This time Monaco seemed to be counting on Anthony and no one would regret it …

Chapter 14

The click

No goals and no assists. This was Anthony's gloomy record going in to the ninth match of the Ligue 1 season, which saw AS Monaco facing a tricky trip to Paris Saint-Germain, the French league title-holders. It was Sunday 5 October 2014 and, at first glance, the Martial affair had moved on little since Leonardo Jardim had taken over. He seemingly remained a second choice in the mind of the Portuguese manager, who had preferred the Bulgarian Dimitar Berbatov at the start of the season, usually accompanied up front by the Belgian Yannick Ferreira-Carrasco, the Argentine Lucas Ocampos, or the young French player Valère Germain. And to top it off, Anthony's only start, against Guingamp on 21 September, the fifth round of fixtures, was cut short when he was forced to come off in the 23rd minute after a blow to the head in a clash with an opposing defender. The picture was a sad and worrying one.

There was one person who was not all that worried, however. That was Jardim himself. The former manager of Sporting Lisbon began paying particular attention to Anthony Martial. 'As soon as he took over the team, he took a great interest in the young players, and in Anthony in particular,' explains Anthony De Freitas, who now plays in the Portuguese league. 'He helped him make a lot of progress off the ball as well as in coming back to defend.

He never let up on him and helped him move up a level, that's for sure.' This opinion is shared by the journalist Fabien Pigalle: 'I don't think he was particularly fond of Anthony, but he spotted enormous potential in him quickly and did everything he could to get as much out of him as possible every day at training.' Chief scout at OL and a former international, Florian Maurice, is on the same wave length: 'Rémi Garde at Lyon and then Claudio Ranieri in that first year in Monaco started to get him to understand things and to give him the foundations to allow him to evolve in the world of professional football, but Jardim, who also took an educational approach, showed him how to put this to work on a daily basis and helped him become a real professional.'

On Sunday 5 October 2014, Anthony would show French football that he really did have the stuff champions are made of. When he was brought on in the 75th minute it was neither a cause for frustration nor the source of a punishment, as it had been in Nantes at the start of the season. This time, these short fifteen minutes spent on the pitch at the Parc des Princes allowed him to snatch an equaliser in the 90th minute thanks to a monumental scramble in the PSG box: after a move initiated by Kurzawa on the left, Anthony rediscovered his goal-scoring instinct, and, with a subtle right-footed swipe, picked up the ball on the bounce and tricked PSG's Italian keeper, Salvatore Sirigu. This time Anthony was able to let out his joy and it showed with a broad smile. He allowed his team to keep the Parisian onslaught at bay with a 1-1 draw. A first step had been taken, but it was too soon to talk about things clicking into place just yet. The following months would confirm that Anthony still had work to do: he played a key role once again on 25 October at Bastia during the eleventh match of the season, this time providing an assist for Ferreira-Carrasco. Despite this, he did not quite manage to convince his coach to put his faith in him more regularly and, more often than not, he found himself on the substitutes' bench.

The click, if it can be called that, came during November at an impromptu visit by the France national team coach to the AS Monaco training centre. Didier Deschamps had already been following Martial's evolution for two seasons since catching him by chance in a famous match for the France Under-19 team. After the match, he is said to have said to his entourage about Anthony: 'There is only one player in this team who has the level to be an international and that's him.' This time the manager of the Bleus spoke directly to the young French striker. In a conversation summarised for the *Agence France-Presse* by Anthony Martial himself: 'He told me I had the talent to do great things, but that I needed to work hard at training for it to pay off.' Of course, the advice given by Deschamps was not enough to transform Anthony overnight. First and foremost, the manager's words reinforced the comments he was receiving on a daily basis from Jardim, and confirmed to Anthony that he would have to work much harder to impose himself in Monaco.

The months of December and January were marked predominantly by this recognition in Anthony's mind, and a taster of what Europe would discover later in the season was being revealed. Between 2 December 2014 and 17 January 2015, ASM's number 23 strung together six consecutive first team starts, four as a centre-forward and two on the right wing: 'It was one of Jardim's bright ideas to put Anthony on the wing,' confirms the journalist Fabien Pigalle. 'This allowed him to learn how to pitch

in defensively and to become a more complete player.'
Whatever the case, it worked: Monaco pulled off five victories and only one draw in these six Ligue 1 fixtures and
Anthony delivered two assists for Berbatov at Toulouse
(5 December) and for Bernardo Silva against Olympique
Marseille (14 December). He was also getting noticed
in the domestic cups by transforming his assists into a
goal against Lyon in the last sixteen of the League Cup
(17 December), then scoring again in the next round, the
quarter-final, in the 2-0 win over Guingamp on 14 January
2015. He ended January and began February with two more
goals, this time in the Coupe de France. On 21 January, in
a last sixteen match at Évian Thonon Gaillard, he brought
an end to the suspense by scoring a goal with his right foot
to make it 2-0, before doing himself justice on 11 February
in the quarter-final at Rennes by converting a penalty he
had won during a 3-1 win over the Breton team. Anthony
was in superb form and it was well timed for the Champions
League quarter-final …

The end of February marked the return of the world's
greatest club competition. That year, 2014–15, AS Monaco
managed to top Group C ahead of Bayer Leverkusen, Zenit
Saint Petersburg and Benfica. This first place finish would
guarantee that Monaco would play the return leg of their
quarter-final at home and that they would face a second-
place team. The draw chose Arsenal as their opponents, a
club that always did well against French teams.

Anthony was kept well away from all these considera-
tions. He was waiting in the starting blocks. He had played
little in the first half of the competition (three matches
out of six), although he had been able to take advantage
of two injuries to Berbatov against Benfica and Zenit
Saint Petersburg to come on earlier than planned in both

matches. This time he seemed to have a real part to play, all the more so because his manager had planned a little surprise for the Gunners in the first leg on 25 February 2015 in London. Anthony made his first start in a Champions League match. But when the players came out onto the pitch, he was neither in the centre-forward position nor on the right wing, where he had already played several times that season, but on the left wing in place of Ferreira-Carrasco, who had been relegated to the bench. It may have been a surprise but it was a strong decision by the Portuguese manager who had also put Berbatov up front and the captain, Nabil Dirar, in a more defensive position on the right wing.

It was a brand new formation that caused Arsenal no end of trouble. The north London team were much more confident before the match and hoped to take advantage of the first leg to make the difference. But they came up against a Monegasque wall that was as solid as the principality's rock. Arsenal also became acquainted with a bulldozer on the left wing: Martial stood out for the first time in the fourteenth minute on the end of a cross from Touré, but the one-two with Elderson Echiéjilé was not to be. Never mind ... it was only a matter of time. In the 35th minute, Martial sent a worrying shiver down the spines of the English fans: he was on the left wing and made the most of his technique to pass Koscielny and Cazorla with a magnificent double touch. He brought his move to an end with an accurate cross to Moutinho who failed to control the pass.

The director of the TV stream was right to pick a close-up of the number 23 to highlight that particular move by Monaco, who were playing in blue that night. The slow motion provided a better look at the young hopeful's sequence. From then on, the crowd at the Emirates Stadium were fearful every time Martial was on the ball. Although he did not play a part in Kondogbia's 38th minute goal, he of course ran over to congratulate his fellow French team player on his successful strike from an ideal position. Monaco were 1-0 up and continued their demonstration in the second half in front of a completely dumbfounded crowd. In the 53rd minute, Anthony once again made the difference on the left wing. He slipped away from his marker on the touch line and saw Berbatov with his sights on goal eighteen metres out. The pass was majestic and the Bulgarian fired past the keeper, Ospina, despite the arrival of three defenders. 2-0 and Anthony's first assist. It was like a dream … or almost. In the 61st minute, Anthony was centimetres away from his first Champions League goal … on a clever backheel from Moutinho, he was a hair's breadth from stalling the advance of Ospina, who eventually deflected the ball for a corner.

Anthony gave up his place to Bernardo Silva in the 84th minute and almost everyone in the crowd had been impressed with his performance and saw strong similarities with another French player, who had also come through Les Ulis and Monaco and brought plenty of happiness to Arsenal for many seasons. Comparisons with Thierry Henry came quickly after the match and it was true that Anthony had been impossible to stop in this particular game. He had the ability to make the difference at every turn. He had made a sudden jump up the ladder. He had been almost the sixth choice striker when he arrived in Monaco a year earlier but now he had become a powerful first team player. Anthony's performance had impressed his teammates, who were invited in turn to have their say on his potential to various media representatives. 'He is a player who, if he is physically and mentally fit, has the qualities to become a great player at European and even world level,' confirmed João Moutinho, while Dimitar Berbatov recognised that 'if he listens to the manager and continues to work as hard in training, he will be one of the best, without a doubt.'

Just like his team, Anthony struggled a little more in the second match played at the Stade Louis II on 17 March 2015. Back on the left wing, he spent much of his time defending against repeated assaults from the Gunners. In the end, Arsenal won 2-0, but thanks to the away goals rule, ASM's 3-1 victory in the first leg saw them through to the Champions League quarter-final. On leaving the stadium, Monaco's supporters were relieved and still enchanted by the performance in the first leg, which had, among other things, revealed Anthony Martial's talent: 'We're really happy we kept him,' confirmed a supporter for the TV microphones and cameras. 'Particularly because if Falcao had stayed, Martial would have gone to Valencia,' concluded another supporter. 'I don't think we lost out, quite the opposite, we're delighted he's still in our team.'

There was no question of back-pedalling now. Anthony would surf this growing wave of popularity to confirm in match after match that he had become AS Monaco's number one asset. In the French league, defences were discovering a different player every weekend. Having stayed silent in Ligue 1 for almost five months, with eighteen strikes but not even a single goal, he was now finding the back of the net at almost every attempt. He scored four league goals in March alone, as well as proving himself for the France Under-21 team, with which he took advantage of a friendly against Holland to score another two goals on 30 March. In April, he kept up his rhythm by equalising with his left foot against AS Saint-Étienne in the 31st fixture of the season, before scoring with his right in the next match, a convincing win at Caen.

Anthony was on a roll and the whole of Monaco was counting on him for the Champions League quarter-final against Juventus. Qualification against Arsenal had had an ultra-positive effect on the players, who were confident about bringing down the Italian champions. During the first match at Juventus Stadium, Anthony was again head and shoulders above the rest. On Tuesday 14 April 2015, he was ready on several occasions to swing the match in favour of ASM. He posed big problems for the Italian defence, which he was taking on full-face this time from the centre-forward position usually occupied by Berbatov. In the tenth minute, he turned on a burst of speed and set his sights on the defence before providing Ferreira-Carrasco with a perfect assist. But the Belgian saw his shot miraculously blocked by Buffon. Anthony kept his chin up and allowed himself another top-flight move in the first half. In the 39th minute, he got the better of Chiellini and the Italian had no option but to throw him off balance right in the middle of the box. Penalty? No, the referee did not blow his whistle despite the Juventus defender's clear foul. These two moves were turning points in this two-leg tie against the Italians. Juventus won the first leg – on a penalty converted by Vidal – and managed to hold on to their narrow advantage in a return leg in which Anthony Martial, like the rest of his team, was rendered powerless and unable to get the better of the Turin defence.

Obviously, elimination in the quarter-final of the Champions League was a blow to Anthony. But it did not stop him finishing the season like a cannonball, scoring two more goals in the French league over the following weeks.

His second year on the Monaco Rock had been the source of many questions early in the season. Twelve months later and all the doubts had been lifted by an incredible 2015. In less than five months, Anthony had become AS Monaco's number one striker.

Chapter 15

A busy summer

The news came in a simple message posted at 4.23 pm on AS Monaco's official Twitter account. It was 26 June 2015. Anthony's face appeared on a red background with the club's logo and the succinct caption: 'Martial until 2019.'

It was accompanied by a brief explanation: 'AS Monaco are delighted to announce that @AnthonyMartial's contract has been extended until 2019 #Martial2019.'

The story was soon picked up by all the French and international media. Reactions followed with the hashtag #Martial2019: 'That's perfect. You'll smash everyone next season', 'That's great news. A big name staying put', 'Congratulations, we're counting on you' and 'We know we're going to have a great future thanks to you'. Messages of encouragement from anonymous fans, and even a photo tweeted by his teammate and captain, Jérémy Toulalan, who showed his satisfaction by posting a picture of a freshly opened bottle of champagne!

It was not hard to understand that this contract extension was great news and a big relief for the club only three days before the resumption of training after the off-season break. The end of the 2014–15 season had left its mark in people's minds and given Anthony an entirely different status in the principality. He was also the symbol of a new policy of recruiting new players that had worked and would continue throughout the summer with the arrival of several great hopes for French football, such as Thomas Lemar, Farès Bahlouli, Corentin Jean and Allan Saint-Maximin.

Shortly afterwards, that afternoon, initial reactions began to arrive. On the official ASM website Anthony confirmed how proud he was to be staying in 'red and white': 'We had a great season last year, and next season is also going to be very exciting. I hope to have a good campaign and repay the faith that's been shown in me.' Alongside him in the photo, holding a 'Martial 2019' shirt, Vadim Vasilyev said: 'It's already impressive, what Anthony is capable of at nineteen years of age, but the best is yet to come.' The Monaco vice-president was particularly happy to be putting an end to a tricky question that had been being asked since early June: Anthony wanted to receive a significant pay rise after his 2014–15 season (twelve goals and five assists in all competitions). According to *L'Équipe*, the two parties had initially had trouble coming to an agreement before ASM's directors put an end to the power struggle under the scrutiny of a number of European suitors (Valencia, Manchester United, Tottenham, Arsenal, Everton and Wolfsburg).

Three days later, Anthony appeared with his teammates on the pitches of the La Turbie training centre for the start of the new 2015–16 season. There was no time to lose for AS Monaco, who were preparing for a busy summer with two Champions League qualifying rounds – ASM had finished third in the French league behind PSG and Olympique Lyonnais, who qualified automatically. The first stage of their preparation was disrupted by a merry-go-round of arrivals and departures, however. It was hard to get a real grasp of AS Monaco's plans: in midfield Geoffrey Kondogbia, the revelation of the previous season's Champions League, left for Serie A to Inter Milan, while up front, Valère Germain (on loan to OGC Nice), Lucas Ocampos (Olympique Marseille) and in particular, Dimitar Berbatov (free transfer), Radamel Falcao (this time on loan to Chelsea) and Yannick Ferreira-Carrasco (transferred for €20 million to Atlético Madrid) had already left the club by early July. In order to replace all these potential first team players, AS Monaco set its sights on the young French players Thomas Lemar (SM Caen) and Farès Bahlouli (Olympique Lyonnais), as well as some foreign hopefuls, the Croat Mario Pašalić (on loan from Chelsea), the Argentine Guido Carrillo (Estudiantes), the Portuguese Ivan Cavaleiro (Benfica) and the Italian striker, Stephan El Shaarawy, on loan for a season from AC Milan. They were all young hopefuls but there were no guarantees that AS Monaco would qualify for the new Champions League season in a few weeks' time. 'Anthony was happy with the new recruits,' explains Mathieu Faure. 'He had even pushed for his friends Thomas Lemar and Farès Bahlouli to come and the club had looked favourably on his request because they wanted to put him in the best frame of mind and give him some responsibility.'

Despite this, it did not stop some of the long-standing more senior members of the Monaco team questioning the consistency of the club's plans: 'We were expecting some players to leave but definitely not so many,' the captain Jérémy Toulalan revealed during an interview with the local press. 'It was easy to understand the questions coming from Toulalan, or even Moutinho, who had decided to stay,' explains the *Monaco-Matin* journalist Fabien Pigalle. 'It's true that at that point in the season, it looked as if everyone had been sold. Lots of players had already been transferred and there were rumours about Martial, Abdennour and Kurzawa.'

It was amid all this uncertainty and constant comings-and-goings that Monaco began their preparation campaign. Anthony was quiet during two friendly matches played against Hannover and Shakhtar Donetsk in the Lublin Cup in Poland. He also failed to score during the two following matches against Dynamo Moscow and Queens Park Rangers. He did eventually find the path to goal during the two final preparation matches, scoring once right at the end of the match against PSV Eindhoven (3-1), and then twice on 22 July 2015 against FSV Mainz 05 in a dazzling 5-1 win.

Six days later, on 28 July, ASM Monaco began their marathon to reach the Champions League. Their first opponents in the third preliminary round were the Swiss team Young Boys from Bern. The first match at the Stade de Suisse was a mere formality. AS Monaco won 3-1. Anthony delivered an assist to Mario Pašalić in the 75th minute. During the return leg a week later, at the Stade Louis II, Monaco inflicted another beating on the Swiss club, this time winning 4-0 with Anthony's first goal of the season. These two official matches removed some of the doubts as to the quality of the squad and reassured fans and players alike, but also confirmed the importance of Martial in Leonardo Jardim's system. The new dimension acquired by Anthony could also be seen in the French league during the first day of the Ligue 1 season on 8 August 2015. In the 'Côte d'Azur derby' against Monaco's neighbours OGC Nice, Anthony supplied Pašalić with another assist. The season seemed to get off to a good start, but for the summer to have been a complete success, they now needed to get past Valencia CF, ASM's final opponents in their quest for the Champions League.

Blocking their way to the main draw, this time the

opposition was an entirely different prospect to the Swiss Young Boys. Valencia were regulars in the competition since the club had reached the final twice in 2000 and 2001. For Anthony, the match took on an added dimension: as against Juventus in the previous season's quarter-final, he found himself face to face with one of the teams he had almost joined just a year ago.

The first leg took place on Wednesday 19 August 2015 in front of more than 40,000 spectators at the Mestalla Stadium. Unsurprisingly, Martial would start the match as centre-forward, as he had the previous season against Arsenal and Juventus; he was not overawed by the import-ance of the occasion. As at the Emirates in London and the Juventus Stadium, he would cause the Spanish club's defenders endless trouble. He had become AS Monaco's X factor, with whom anything could happen. Yet again, he was very good against Valencia, a cut above, especially in the second half, in which he tore them apart, forcing them to put four or five players on him. Monaco went 1-0 down in the fourth minute, but, despite starting badly, Jardim's play-ers did everything they could to get back on track. Anthony was involved in every single move: in the 33rd minute, he picked up the ball and began a counter-attack supported by Bernardo Silva before controlling the ball just outside the area and unleashing a cross … it was deflected onto the post by the keeper, Matthew Ryan. Six minutes later the back of the net was finally shaking: Anthony was on the receiving end of a pass from Fabinho and took no time at all in scoring with his right foot … goal disallowed for an off-side position. There was no question of giving up, he gave more and more and remained a constant thorn in Valencia's side during the second half. In the 49th minute, he dribbled the ball with his left foot before making a clever pass to Pašalić. 1-1. Monaco had recovered from the deficit and Anthony kept on going. He was relentless during the final 30 minutes at the Mestalla: he was constantly goading his opponents, taking them on, crossing … He resisted, got in between them and sometimes finished with a strike, but without success. In the meantime, Valencia scored two further goals thanks to their captain Daniel Parejo and play-maker Sofiane Feghouli. 3-1. It was clearly a great result for the team from La Liga, who, without having to show too much of what they could do, already had one foot in the Champions League.

Before the return leg at the Stade Louis II on 25 August, the journalists were unanimous: the situation was almost desperate, unless Martial could pull off a miracle. This was the opinion of the French columnist Pierre Ménès, among others: 'After how well he played in the away leg, the France Under-21 player could change the direction of the match on his own. In any case, ASM will need Martial to be at the peak of his powers to turn over the deficit.' In the end, Anthony and Monaco would fail to turn the match around. But they were not far away from doing so. Quickly behind on the scoreboard yet again, this time to a goal from Begredo, they would score twice thanks to Raggi (from a Martial cross) and Echiéjilé in the final fifteen minutes. Two goals were not enough to bring down Valencia.

Monaco had failed and would not play in the Champions League that season. The principality's club would have to content itself with the Europa League for the 2015–16 season. Not quite the same level of prestige. A few days from the end of the transfer window, ASM were preparing for an uncertain end to the summer. However, after the two matches against Valencia, there was one player who had not lost everything.

Anthony's smile would return only two days after the Champions League elimination: on Thursday, 27 August, in the early afternoon, he received a phone call from his father, Florent. It was not to cheer him up but to give him some very important news: he had been called up to the France team for the first time for two friendly matches planned for 4 and 7 September against Portugal and Serbia. In the press conference, Didier Deschamps had no trouble justifying his selection: 'He can play in the centre or on the wing. He also has power and speed. He's a young player but he has an interesting profile in an area of the pitch where these qualities are not easy to find. He has great potential. We'll see how he gets on in the squad.' The first official comments would come from Anthony Martial later that day on the ASM website: 'Wearing the France shirt is really a huge source of pride and I hope to do well. Every player dreams of representing their country, and now it's my turn, so I'm very happy. Now it's up to me to work hard and earn regular call-ups. It is a new step and it's been my ambition since I was very young.' Anthony ended the interview by mentioning the highlight of the French league calendar that was due to take place three days later on Sunday, 30 August at Parc des Princes against PSG: 'Now we need to focus on producing a big performance against PSG, and put the disappointment against Valencia behind us.' He did not know yet that his team would be soundly beaten 3-0 in the fourth match of the league season. But did he already know it would be his last 90 minutes in an AS Monaco shirt?

Chapter 16

The longest day

At 11 am he climbed the stairs of the château at Clairefontaine, but his suitcase stayed in the car. It was Monday, 31 August 2015, the first day of the France national team training camp to prepare for the friendlies against Portugal and Serbia. It was Anthony Martial's first time with Les Bleus. But it was not to be a first time like many others. The usual rules of the game did not apply to this nineteen-year-old. Martial had come to the training centre in Yvelines to ask for permission to get on a plane. Never in the history of the French Football Federation had a player left a training camp to close a transfer. But given the 'exceptional circumstances', after speaking with the federation bosses and Louis van Gaal, manager of the Red Devils, Didier Deschamps, the France team coach, granted Martial permission to travel to Manchester. 'It's a question of making a choice for his career. I'm not here to make the situation more difficult for players and clubs interested in buying them,' justified Deschamps. 'There are players who go to other clubs and other countries, it seems normal to me to make it easier for them to pass the medical. The transfer window closes on Monday night in France, tomorrow in England. If the same thing happened with another player, I would act the same way.'

At noon, the Monaco forward left Clairefontaine. Half an hour later, a press release from the federation made his departure official and explained that he was expected to return on Tuesday morning. It was the confirmation on which the transfer rumours, which had started circulating at around midday on 30 August, were based. It was the confirmation that the deal was on the table.

At 12.48 pm, accompanied by Philippe Lamboley, his agent, and Afif Mshangama, his lawyer, Anthony took off for England. Newspaper websites in France and England went crazy, summing up the whole story, or to put it better, what they knew about the story. On Sunday, AS Monaco was said to have received an astonishing offer from Manchester United for the young forward: €50 million. Vadim Vasilyev, vice-president of ASM, initially rejected the offer. He also said no to €70 million. But as we all know, in Monaco, and in football in general, nothing is impossible. So much so that at 1.21 pm on Monday, the press agencies announced that the two clubs had come to an agreement for the transfer of Anthony Martial. There was talk of €80 million, including bonuses, a figure that would turn out to be true. The contract in its entirety, published on 16 January 2016 by the website Football Leaks, revealed that AS Monaco received €50 million payable in two parts: €20 million on approval of the contract by the Premier League and the remaining €30 million before 1 July 2016.

Added to this sum were bonuses linked to player performance, which could reach another €30 million: €10 million if Martial scored 25 goals in official games for Manchester United, another €10 million if he played 25 games (at least 45 minutes per match) for the French national team, and a further €10 million if he was nominated for the Ballon d'Or while wearing a Manchester United shirt. That was not all: in addition to the three bonuses, the contract included a clause that would force Manchester United to split the surplus 50/50 with Monaco if they sold Martial for at least €60 million.

These were the figures and clauses of which, at 1.21 pm on 31 August, no one except the interested parties was aware. But the bomb had gone off. On both sides of the Channel, nobody could talk about anything other than the crazy amount paid for a nineteen-year-old boy who had only played 52 Ligue 1 matches, scored 11 goals and not yet played for the France team.

The €80 million would make Martial the world's most expensive teenage footballer and the sixth most expensive player in the history of football after Cristiano Ronaldo (from Manchester United to Real Madrid, in 2009, €94 million), Gareth Bale (from Tottenham to Real Madrid, in 2013, €91 million), Neymar (from Santos to FC Barcelona, in 2013, €86 million), Luis Suárez (from Liverpool to Barcelona, in 2014, €81 million) and James Rodríguez (from Monaco to Real Madrid, in 2014, €80 million). More expensive even than Zinedine Zidane, who went from Juventus to Real Madrid for €75 million in 2001 (although in that case the contract did not include any bonuses). €5 million more than the most expensive player in the history of French football, but Zizou, unlike Martial, could boast the titles of world champion (1998), European champion (2000) and even a Ballon d'Or (1998). A lot of water may well have gone under the bridge since then, figures kept on multiplying, but comparisons always have an impact. Martial had become United's second most expensive signing after Angel Di Maria (£59.7m), not to mention the fact that he was clearly the most expensive purchase in the 2015 transfer market: he beat Kevin de Bruyne, the 25-year-old Belgian, who was sold by VfL Wolfsburg to Manchester City for €75 million.

The €80 million for Martial made the front pages of the newspapers and was analysed in a thousand different ways. For example, with two very simple divisions: €80m/11 = €7.27 million per goal scored; €80m/52 = €1.538m, more than €1.5 million per match. Comparisons were also made with the transfer fees of other young talented players, such as Wayne Rooney, who joined United in 2004 at the age of eighteen after playing 67 matches for Everton in the Premier League and scoring fifteen goals. The captain of the England team had cost 'only' €30 million. Or Karim Benzema, aged 21, who went from Olympique Lyonnais to Real Madrid for €35 million in 2009. And Thierry Henry, transferred from Monaco to Juventus for €12.5 million in 1999. Not to mention Cristiano Ronaldo, who went to Manchester United from Sporting Lisbon for €15 million at the age of eighteen. Example after example of players who already had a good track record with a World Cup in their pocket (Henry), or the title of best player in Ligue 1 (Benzema), who were sold for up to seven times less than Martial (in the case of Henry). So much so that the BBC unearthed a study carried out by the Soccerex Football Value Index that assessed Martial's real value at €13.7 million. This was not far off the conclusions made by the Observatory of the International Centre for Sports Studies (CIES) in a report on over-valued players: Martial should have cost the Red Devils no more than €22.1 million.

The stratospheric figure that had broken the transfer market bank certainly provided plenty to talk about. It was the topic of the day at Clairefontaine. At 4.33 pm, at the afternoon press conference, Didier Deschamps, like it or not, was forced to have his say. 'These are very big sums. He is a player with huge potential. Everything has moved very fast for him since he left Lyon in 2013. Today's transfer fees

MERCI AUX CHAMPIONS DU MONDE U20

(above) Martial lining up for France's U21s ahead of a UEFA European U21 Championships qualifier against Kazakhstan U21s in September 2013. Back row, far right.

CHARLY TRIBALLEAU/AFP/ Getty Images

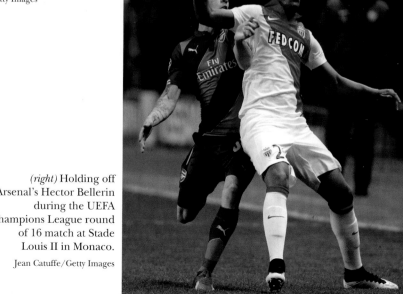

(right) Holding off Arsenal's Hector Bellerin during the UEFA Champions League round of 16 match at Stade Louis II in Monaco.

Jean Catuffe/Getty Images

(above) Making his senior debut for France in a friendly against Portugal in September 2015.

Carlos Rodrigues/Getty Images

(left) Martial is unveiled by Manchester United on 1 September 2015 following his £36 million transfer from AS Monaco.

John Peters/Man Utd via Getty Images

(above) Martial scores on his debut for Manchester United in a 3-1 win over bitter rivals Liverpool in the Barclays Premier League.

Matthew Peters/Man Utd via Getty Images

(right) An injury-time strike from Martial in the Emirates FA Cup semi-final against Everton sends Manchester United through to the final.

Matthew Ashton/AMA/ Getty Images

(*above*) Martial celebrates victory after the Emirates FA Cup final against Crystal Palace. Man Utd won 2-1 after extra time.

Paul Gilham/Getty Images

(*left*) Martial is consoled by Paul Pogba after France's 0-1 defeat against Portugal in the UEFA Euro 2016 final at Stade de France on 10 July 2016.

Lars Baron/Getty Images

can be massive, but it's less risky to invest in a young player than an older one. He's signing for a massive club. He will be on another planet, in another galaxy! It's up to him to continue his development and gain some time on the pitch. Time will tell if he has made the right choice.' When they ask him if United was taking a big risk by gambling on a player who had yet to prove what he could do, the France manager replied sternly: 'Transfers are not gambles but investments. When Monaco bought Martial for 5 million from Lyon, everyone wondered why. How much is he worth now? Some clubs, managers and coaches see a player and think he has potential, room for improvement in anticipation of a capital gain. As far as the public are concerned, these are huge sums. If we look outside the world of football, it's a disproportionate sum but given the means of clubs like Manchester United, it's not that significant.'

And finally, a question about Martial beating Zidane's record? This seemed unbelievable to the journalists but not to Deschamps: 'Other players will go on to beat the record. The transfer is colossal but that's the reality today. Transfer records were also being beaten fifteen years ago. Modern football generates more and more money. What can we do about it? English clubs now have colossal resources at their disposal. When they want a player, French clubs or clubs in other countries can't refuse.' As far as Vadim Vasilyev was concerned, the French national team manager was spot on: 'The other transfers were more or less expected,' explained the Russian president, 'but not Anthony's. We extended his contract in July because we thought the 2015–16 season would be his. Martial was not for sale, but since last week United started to make offers which we declined several times – £21.6m, £28.8m, £36m, even £50.4m with bonuses. Finally United made an offer which the club couldn't refuse. It's absolutely unique. It's the price of Luis Suárez or Neymar, the best players in the world. Right now English football is on a different financial level and if Manchester United decides to buy somebody, it's very hard to stop them.' There is no doubt that the economic power of the Premier League, thanks to television rights valued at €7 billion for the period from 2016 to 2019, is immense. According to a study carried out by Deloitte, it allowed English clubs to spend more than €1 billion in the summer transfer window. It also allowed United to pay 'a bit extra' for the Monaco striker. Because, as Van Gaal would explain: 'The fee reflected a trend of United routinely being quoted £10m more for players than other clubs.'

Good value for Manchester United and a good deal for Monaco: they paid €5 million and took home €50 million, not to mention the bonuses. But unlike the executives at the principality's club, who were delighted at their full coffers, many players were puzzled. This was true of the captain Jérémy Toulalan, who declared: 'We were expecting some players to leave, but not so many.' It was a sign that in Monaco, once the transfer window had opened, everyone had a price, anyone could be sold, even rough diamonds like Martial could end up on the market. From a sporting point of view, Monaco were heavily criticised because they failed to move to replace what they had lost or to strengthen the ASM squad. Dissenting voices could also be heard regarding the size of the deal: they could have waited to sell him given that they had already collected €150 million in transfer fees. They could have waited for him to mature for one more year in the red and white shirt, ensuring that offers for Martial in 2016 would have been even more enticing.

But of course, ifs, maybes and buts don't count. The die had been cast.

At 5.33 pm on Monday, 31 August, Anthony Martial underwent the customary medical examination at United's Carrington training centre. It was supposed to be the last step before the contract was signed, but that was not the case: negotiations between the former Lyonnais player's entourage and the powers that be at Manchester United, which had begun at 6.30 pm, dragged on until 3 am. Ed Woodward, the executive vice-chairman of the club on one side, Philippe Lamboley and Afif Mshangama on the other, negotiated the contract between the player and the club. It would last for four years, plus one further optional year (2019–20), with a net monthly salary of €380,000, a bonus of €1 million for Champions League qualification, a €150,000 performance-related bonus, and further bonuses for achieving particular objectives. The interminable negotiations also included a discussion of the finer details to make sure the newly arrived player could settle in in the best way possible: a driver to help him get around given that Anthony did not have a driving licence, a personal assistant who would help him find somewhere to live in Manchester and solve any day-to-day problems with life in England, and his own English teacher to help him get to grips with the new language. The United representatives wanted their new Golden Boy to concentrate on football and football alone. While the negotiations were going on, Martial had time to visit the facilities at Carrington and to meet Louis van Gaal. The manager explained his footballing philosophy, told him what was expected of him and asked him in which position he preferred to play. 'In the centre,' Anthony replied. 'You'll play in several positions,' came the Dutch coach's response. His number was also decided:

the number 9 had remained vacant since Radamel Falcao had left for Chelsea. It was a legendary number for the Red Devils, worn by Sir Bobby Charlton as well as Denis Law and George Best, the United trinity. Sir Bobby Charlton wore it from 1956 to 1973. United's executives had the club store opened at 4 am so Anthony could be immortalised in the number 9 red shirt.

On Tuesday, 1 September at midday, just in time for lunch, Martial arrived back at Clairefontaine. He made his first announcement on the French federation website: 'It was a restless night. But I'm very happy to sign for Manchester United. It's a very big club and I hope I'll be able to show all my qualities. There's certainly been a lot of talk about it, but the most important thing will be on the pitch and to show people who I am. You have to stay true to yourself and keep your head on your shoulders.'

6.14 pm, one hour before the closure of the summer transfer window in England:

> '#mufc is pleased to announce French forward @AnthonyMartial has completed his transfer from Monaco. #WelcomeMartial'

This tweet from Manchester United was accompanied by a snapshot of Martial in a blue tracksuit against a black background printed with logos of the club and sponsors. The boy is holding on tightly to a United shirt with both hands.

6.16 pm, confirmation from Monaco: 'AS Monaco and @ManUtd have come to an agreement for the transfer of @AnthonyMartial. The club wishes him all the best for the future.'

6.17 pm, another tweet, this time from Martial:

'I am so excited to be joining Manchester United. I have enjoyed my time at AS Monaco and I would like to thank them and the fans for everything they have done for me. I have always wanted to play in the Premier League and to join the biggest club in the world is what every young footballer dreams of. I am looking forward to meeting my new teammates and working with Louis van Gaal who has achieved so much in his career.'

Two minutes later it was the turn of Louis van Gaal: 'Anthony is a talented young forward with great potential. I believe this is the club for him to continue his development.'

Chapter 17

Anthony who?

'On the plane Wayne Rooney came to speak to me and asked me who Martial was, because the English press had started to speak about him. I told him he's a great player with great potential, who has played some good matches with Monaco last season and the beginning of this. I told him he is technical and powerful. A little like Thierry Henry, even if it's the press who are making that comparison.' The anecdote was recounted by Morgan Schneiderlin, the French defender who had joined Manchester United in July 2015. The scene unfolded on a flight carrying United home from Swansea on the evening of 30 August after the Red Devils had fallen to their first defeat of the season (2-1). Apparently the England captain and United's star player was curious (and interested given that his position up front could be in the balance) to find out about this nineteen-year-old kid who the papers were already linking to the north-east club. There was no doubt that Rooney was not the only one who did not know Anthony Martial.

'When the news of his purchase broke, no one, or almost no one, had any idea who the Monaco player was. Who? Anthony who? Everyone was asking,' explained James Taylor, journalist for the *Manchester Evening News*. 'Perhaps some managers and scouts had heard of him, but they probably wouldn't have been able to recognise his face. The same was true of the journalists and fans. In England, we follow the Champions League, the big clubs in the Spanish *liga*, German and Italian clubs, but to be honest we don't follow Ligue 1 much. So everyone was wondering who he was, because United had spent an enormous sum of money for a teenager, and what such a young player with so little experience could bring to the club. There was a huge amount of scepticism about the kid's arrival.' In the United Kingdom, the theory that the purchase of the most expensive teenager in the history of British football had been a question of panic buying began to take hold. Angel Di Maria, Radamel Falcao and Robin van Persie had left and the top names many were fantasising about (from Cristiano Ronaldo to Edinson Cavani, from Neymar to Benzema, from Thomas Müller to Gareth Bale, not forgetting Robert Lewandowski) had never arrived, leaving United wiped out. And after a disappointing start to the season, in the last five days of the transfer window, they were in a desperate panic for a striker, a super-player who would make the difference in one-on-ones. There was no time to lose, United were not short of money and they had decided to play the roulette wheel in Monte Carlo: €80 million for some almost unknown guy. The rumour in the principality claimed that the proof was in the fact that even once the deal had been done, Manchester United scouts kept calling Monaco for information about the player. They wanted to know what he was like off the pitch, if he was married, if he had children, how he behaved in the dressing room, if he could speak English … they needed to write a report for Van Gaal and they needed information. Just as the Man Utd captain had asked his French teammate to shed some light.

'That's not what happened. The story has been blown out of proportion,' maintains Lamboley, Martial's agent. 'It was about getting more information, finding out how he played, but that doesn't mean Rooney didn't know who he was. He had already seen him play but didn't follow him regularly. Honestly, I think that in the world of football, anyone who had seen Anthony play in big matches like those against Arsenal or Juventus, immediately realised how much he was worth.' This explains why he was under surveillance by the cream of European clubs, from Barça to PSG, from Tottenham to Chelsea. Roman Abramovich's club was said to have offered Monaco a fee higher than that of Manchester United, without bonuses. And that agreement would have seen Martial spend another year in the principality. But in the end the deal was not done because 'Anthony wanted to go to Manchester, it was his childhood dream. If we'd killed that dream', Vadim Vasilyev told *Le Journal de Dimanche*, 'we could have lost the boy for several months. He sent me his first autographed jersey and thanked me for giving him this chance.'

'He could have gone to Spain, but the Premier League was the league he wanted to play in and Manchester United was the club he loved,' confirmed Lamboley, not at all surprised by the price paid. 'How can anyone think United would have spent an amount of money like that without knowing the player … They had been following Anthony since his youth football days. As for the price … Nowadays there are lots of examples, De Bruyne, they bought him for €6 million and sold him for €20 million and everyone said it was a good deal for Chelsea. In the end he was sold to Manchester City for €75 million. Juventus sold Kingsley Coman to Bayern with an option of €20 million and they might end up kicking themselves. That's how it is with very young players. And if Anthony becomes one of the top five strikers in the world, what they've paid will be a drop in the ocean.' Not everyone on the other side of the Channel agreed. Starting with Van Gaal, who, in a press conference, called the price paid for the ex-Monaco player 'ridiculous' and saw it as a symptom of the 'crazy world we are in.' The Dutch manager was convinced that the purchase of the nineteen-year-old was a long-term investment: 'I have not bought Martial for me, I have bought him for the next manager of Manchester United.' It would take time for the boy to cut his teeth in the Premier League but this was not a foregone conclusion. There were plenty of doubts about his performance in England. Take Thierry Henry for example, who told *Sky Sports*: 'Can he score a lot of goals? I don't know. It's hard to say because he's only played 52 matches in Ligue 1. It's an enormous gamble. There's a question mark over his ability to develop at that level. He'll have to adapt, but as I said, he's only played 52 matches in Ligue 1. It's unbelievable!'

The former Arsenal player was in good company given that so many French commentators were extremely sceptical about whether the kid from Les Ulis could offer a good account of himself across the Channel. They thought it was a mistake to have embarked on such an adventure and that he would have been much better off if he had stayed in the cocoon of Ligue 1 for a while to develop quietly in the shadow of Monaco's rock. Instead he catapulted himself into one of the world's biggest clubs with everything that brings with it in terms of pressure from fans and the British media.

On Wednesday, 2 September, Anthony Martial took it upon himself to respond to the sceptics, silence his critics and tell things as they really were. It was his first press conference at Clairefontaine, his first in a France shirt, but there was little talk of Les Bleus. Anthony only mentioned that he had sung *Désolé* by the French rap group

Sexion d'Assaut as his initiation and repeated that playing for France was 'a dream'. The journalists' questions then turned to his transfer to Manchester United and the stratospheric figure paid by the English club. 'I don't know if I'm worth €80 million. It's a crazy sum for a player of my age but that's the football market. It's between the two clubs. I'll try not to let myself get distracted and I don't feel under any pressure.' Anthony spoke candidly and then admitted: 'My family were really happy for me that I'm going to such a big club. They were definitely a bit nervous because of my high price but I'm going to stay focused on proving my worth.' What about everyone else? What did his France teammates say about the €80 million? 'Nobody here has talked about the price. They congratulated me and told me not to let it go to my head.' Martial answered firmly, before adding: 'Pat Evra, who lives in the same town as me in France, has only ever had good things to say to me about Manchester United. He told me it was a club of champions, a club that, above all else, wants to win.' Next came the question of risk, an issue with which the French press seemed to be preoccupied: the difficulty a young player would have in leaving the known for the unknown of the Premier League. 'It isn't a risk. I'll be more visible, but if I play like I know I can there's no reason why it shouldn't go well. Ever since I was very young I've been told that I have the characteristics to play in the English league and I'm keen to show my worth. It's going to be a big change from Monaco, the environment and the supporters. In England they really live for football. It's up to me to adapt.'

The journalists had what they needed. Martial continued by talking in detail about the previous week, during which his career as a football player had taken off. He only gave a little clue about his decision: 'It was after we were knocked out of the Champions League [25 August against Valencia] that I decided … When my agent told me that Manchester United wanted to sign me it was a truly exceptional moment for me and I did not hesitate for one second.' Martial had also received a phone call from Louis van Gaal and, since his English was not particularly good, his mother Myriam acted as an interpreter between her son and the manager. In a press conference lasting almost an hour there was of course reference to Rooney's infamous question to Morgan Schneiderlin: 'Anthony who?' Without missing a beat or having prepared a response (at least according to his agent) Anthony replied with a smile: 'It's normal that he doesn't know me. I haven't played that much in Ligue 1 and it's the first time I've been called up to the France team. I will make progress by playing alongside him.' Not even a hint of arrogance, no 'don't you know who I am?', just modesty and calm. The best way to tiptoe into a whole new world.

Chapter 18

A fairy-tale start

The sixty-fifth minute. Anthony Martial is about to make his Premier League debut in the Manchester United number 9 shirt. Someone in the stands holds up a handwritten sign: 'Welcome to the Theatre of Dreams' with five red exclamation marks. He comes on in place of Juan Mata, makes the sign of the cross, points to his teammates to confirm the position he is going to take up, and moves towards the middle of the pitch. All eyes are on him, including the TV camera lenses that show him in close-up while Martin Tyler, the *Sky Sports* commentator, summarises his career from Lyon to Monaco and up to his extraordinary transfer to United. Of course, he stresses the £36 million, which may eventually climb to £57 or £58 million, spent on the French nineteen-year-old. The Red Devils' fans treat 'the most expensive teenager in the world' to a welcoming round of applause.

On 12 September 2015, Old Trafford played host to the fifth match of the season. United were 1-0 up against their arch rivals Liverpool. In the 49th minute, Juan Mata had a free kick just outside the area to the left of the Liverpool goal. Everyone was waiting for him to put in a cross but in the end the Spaniard pulled the ball back across the goal. Daley Blind was unmarked and came running in. He had just enough time to set his sights on target and fired a left-footed shot from eighteen yards out into the far corner of Simon Mignolet's net. A beautiful set piece that was the result of hours of training and enabled the Dutch defender to score his first goal at Old Trafford. Four minutes after coming on, Martial watched the second goal. A wonderful deep pass from Michael Carrick met the onrushing Ander Herrera, who slipped into the right of the area. The Liverpool number 12, Joe Gomez, only eighteen years old, hooked the leg of the Basque player either through inexperience or bad luck. Penalty. It was Herrera himself who took it and he made no mistake, firing the ball under the crossbar. Unstoppable. 2-0. Anthony Martial had yet to touch the ball and would not until the 79th minute when he picked out Marouane Fellaini in a good position, but the Belgian's shot found Martin Škrtel. In the 81st minute, Dejan Lovren offered the new arrival a rich but juicy lesson in what it means to play in the Premier League. The former Monaco player received the ball from Fellaini a few yards inside the opposition half. He tried to get around the Liverpool number 6 with a backheel but he failed. The pair fought for the ball, Anthony defended it, just keeping it inside the sideline. Lovren used his body and leg to tie Anthony up, almost in a wrestling hold, and the United number 9 ended up on the ground. A full-blown welcome to the English league. The referee blew his whistle for the foul against Martial. In the 83rd minute Liverpool pulled one back with a fabulous goal from Christian Benteke. The Belgian number 9, born in Kinshasa, picked up the ball after it rebounded off a United defender in the box and tried an acrobatic overhead kick that fired the ball past De Gea. It was a higher leap and a harder strike than when Wayne Rooney had pulled off the same trick against Manchester City. A masterpiece ... and another would follow only three minutes later.

It was Martial's moment. He got the ball on the left wing,

a fair distance from the goal. Switching into sixth gear he sped past Nathaniel Clyne and Martin Škrtel as if they were slalom poles, and, with a touch of luck, a rebound fell his way and he found himself in front of Mignolet for a right-footed kick towards the far post. It was a great goal right under the Stretford End. 'OHHHH YES!!! WELCOME TO MANCHESTER UNITED, ANTHONY MARTIAL!' shouted Martin Tyler like a madman, while the kid in the number 9 shirt ran along the touchline blowing kisses to the crowd before jumping up and punching the air at the corner flag. It was the same gesture a certain Pelé had made against Sweden in the 1958 World Cup. Under the grandstand, Anthony beat his fists on his chest before being over-whelmed by hugs from his teammates. Old Trafford was in raptures. Martial had finished Liverpool off and, as the *Sky Sports* commentators would say, he had dispelled any doubts in an instant, paid back all the expectations hanging over him with an incredible debut, a moment that would stay in his memory for the rest of his life, not to mention those of the 60,000 people in the stands. 'Forget the second Thierry Henry, this is the first Anthony Martial,' concluded Tyler, while the number 9 escaped from the hugs and made the sign of the cross. What more could you ask from life? First appearance, first goal just 21 minutes after taking to the pitch. One shot, one goal, maximum effectiveness, maxi-mum emotion. 'Luckily I don't have a heart condition!' remembers Florent Martial, who was in the stands that day. 'It was very emotional. He silenced all the critics with that goal.'

'It's true that there was a lot of very negative criticism coming from France,' confirmed Philippe Lamboley. 'They were saying he had made a mistake by going to Manchester, that no one knew him in England, when that wasn't true at all. As soon as he started warming up, the crowd were on their feet cheering. After he scored … in a match like that … it was a super moment, exceptional … Anthony was very happy.'

'I think it was the greatest goal I've ever scored. It was amazing. It just couldn't have been a better way to start. From being a young kid I'd dreamed of playing at Old Trafford and to be able to score in my first game in such a way against such an important opponent, United's biggest rival, it couldn't have turned out any better. It was positive, gave me lots of confidence, it helped me to settle in as a player. Fortunately, things started to go well for me from that moment on and I kept scoring regularly,' the number 9 would say later. It was a goal that would later win him the Manchester United Goal of the Season.

But it was not just him and his entourage who were happy. The stunning debut from the new French kid on the block brought an avalanche of comments. All positive. They came flooding in during the last few minutes of the game and especially after the final whistle. '#Martial wow! What an introduction to @manutd!' said Rio Ferdinand, the ex-United defender. Robbie Savage, formerly of Derby County, replied: 'Millions and millions of pounds, what a bargain! Nineteen years old, to do that on your debut against your side's arch rivals … he slalomed in between so many defenders. What a goal!' After the match when Ashley Young was asked how Martial's English was coming along, the United midfielder replied: 'Morgan Schneiderlin is the translator but if Anthony talks like that on the pitch, that's all we need. Bastian Schweinsteiger, the German world champion, tweeted: 'What a game! Very proud of our team performance. Special congrats to @AnthonyMartial – is there a better way to debut?'

Of course, there was also the judgement of the Dutch manager: 'When you make a goal like Anthony you cannot wish for more I think. He scored a marvellous goal and physically he can play in the Premier League. A lot of players have made a debut and scored with me so it's a good signal,' maintained Van Gaal, who added: 'We have scouted him and we wanted him because he's the best in his age, he needs time. He's been with us for three days, that is too short to judge his personality but he made a very good impression in the first three days, that's why I selected him to be on the bench.'

That's right, Martial had only been training with his new teammates for three days. Before that he had made his debut for the French senior team, on 4 September at the José Alvalade stadium against Cristiano Ronaldo's Portugal. He came on in the 74th minute in a white shirt with a number 20 on his back. Didier Deschamps sent him on in place of Karim Benzema, who had not had a particularly brilliant night and only had a dangerous free kick to his name. The game had stagnated and the scoreboard showed 0-0.

Anthony was in a hurry to pay back his manager's trust and began pressuring the Portuguese defenders two minutes after he came on. In the 79th minute, he picked up a pass from Antoine Griezmann just outside the Portuguese area, but was immediately spotted by Pepe and José Fonte. He lost the ball. Five minutes from the final whistle, Mathieu Valbuena, the OL defender who had come on in the 79th minute, flew a wonderful free kick over Rui Patricio and gave France a victory. Martial? He had had few opportunities to show what he could do, however, at the age of nineteen he had stamped his card with the senior national team for the first time. Afterwards, he offered these impressions in the mixed zone: 'We won, that's the most important thing. I came on and I couldn't be happier. I'm proud that the manager had faith in me. It's a bit like the Champions League, very intense. I gave what I needed to give and we got a win. It's certainly different from the Under 21s and youth teams. I'm very happy to be here and I hope to be called up regularly by playing well for my club.'

His second match for Les Bleus came on Monday, 7 September in Bordeaux in another friendly against Serbia. That Saturday, on the pitch at the Nouveau Stade, Deschamps came over to Martial after the light training session. His tone was decisive and his gestures seemed to point to the fact that the manager was not entirely happy with the striker's work. If truth be told Martial had already been brought into line at the start of the session by Guy Stéphan, Deschamps' number two. It was a scene that had already been played out in football more than once and would be seen an infinite number of times, but it gave the measure of the attention the national team manager was paying to Martial. Many thought he should have been in the starting eleven for the match against Serbia. Didier Deschamps was still thinking it over the day before the match, however: 'It's no small thing starting a match in a France shirt, with all that brings with it on an emotional level.' In the end he decided against it and brought Martial on in the 76th minute for the final quarter of an hour of play. He replaced Valbuena, who went off to applause after what was his 50th cap. The result was 2-1: two goals from Blaise Matuidi and one from Aleksandar Mitrović. Three minutes after coming on, Anthony immediately showed his worth by threading a ball into the area from the left wing. Kondogbia and Benzema were there but they got in each other's way and the move vanished into thin air. In the 83rd minute, Anthony controlled the ball well with his back to goal, went past Tomović and won a foul by the right sideline. Nothing else to report. France played like they hadn't played in a long time and for Martial, a week of madness full of million-pound contracts, national team matches, comments, criticism and the world's attention drew to a close.

He was getting ready to amaze Manchester and United's fans with his incredible goal against Liverpool. Nor would it be the last. Those who thought the young French player was just a flash in the pan would have to think again a few weeks later. Martial continued to amaze, as he did against PSV. It had only been three days since his debut in a red shirt and he already found himself in the starting eleven for the first match in the Champions League Group B game against the Dutch champions. It was a bad night for United, who went down 2-1 and lost Luke Shaw to a broken leg. Martial failed to score but he kept himself busy. The Red Devils' fans were so impressed that they flooded social media with tweets: Nick: 'Martial looked class – really adds another dimension. Promising link-up between him and Memphis too. Lot to be optimistic about there'; Elliott: 'Martial played like our most experienced forward tonight. He's gonna be very good'; Dave: 'Martial absolutely looks the real deal though. Very impressed with his play at times. Going to be a long road for him, but he's "got it"'; Ikaka: 'Anthony Martial was great tonight again. Bright future for him. It's amazing he's just nineteen with so much talent.'

On 20 September, the sixth match of the Premier League season, he was even better. At St Mary's Stadium, Anthony started against Southampton and scored twice: in the 34th minute, with his right foot from the centre of the area to draw level after Graziano Pellè's goal, then, in the 50th minute, he picked up a ball given away by Maya Yoshida and put the Red Devils ahead 3-1. The match finished 3-2 and United climbed to second place in the table, two points behind City. Martial was the man of the match and the third United player to score in his first two Premier League games after Louis Saha in 2014 and Federico Macheda in 2009, although whenever the Italian's name comes up it is often with a note of criticism. Martial, who was intended as a gift for Van Gaal's successor, had become irreplaceable. Even if the Dutch manager was trying to dampen down the enthusiasm: 'A lot of people are thinking he is a great star but he is a boy of nineteen. In three matches he has shown a lot. I am very happy with him but we and he have to keep our feet on the ground.'

23 September, Old Trafford, Capital One Cup, third round. Anthony came on for Mata in the 70th minute against Ipswich. Twenty-two minutes later, he scored the third goal on the end of an assist from Memphis Depay. 3-0 United. The French player's streak continued: four goals in four games. It was hard to remember such an impact from a player who had just arrived in England. Not to mention from a nineteen-year-old. Those that came to mind were Eric Cantona's arrival at Leeds and Manchester United, or Fernando Torres at Anfield, or more recently Alexis Sanchez at Arsenal or Diego Costa at Chelsea. But these were players who could boast plenty of experience, players who had already done their homework and passed exams in leagues elsewhere. No other young, emerging French players arriving in the United Kingdom had momentum that compared to Martial. Take Thierry Henry, he would go on to become a star at Highbury, but the first few months were tough and full of missed opportunities. Or Nicolas Anelka, who would need seven hours of match play before opening his Arsenal account.

There was no doubt that in just four matches the former

Monaco player had impressed everyone. Starting with Sir Alex Ferguson, who said of the Reds' new number 9: 'The boy Anthony Martial, he can be anything. What I like about the boy is that he doesn't panic. I don't think you can teach that.' Thierry Henry shared this opinion. The ex-Gunner, who had been sceptical about the transfer of the boy from Les Ulis, took it all back and told *talkSPORT*: 'What I like about him is how calm he is. It seems like he isn't fazed, he doesn't care what people are talking about, what they are saying, where he is playing, the expectations. When he arrives in front of the goal, he is composed like a striker who has been in the game for six, seven years. So, credit to him.' There were those, such as Jamie Redknapp, former Liverpool and Tottenham midfielder turned *Sky Sports* commentator, who even went so far as to say: 'I watched Anthony Martial for 90 minutes in the Champions League and the only nineteen-year-old I've seen better at that age was Lionel Messi. I played against Wayne Rooney when he made his debut but this boy has so much intelligence. He knows when to pass, when to cross it, when to dribble and when to shoot. He goes past people like they're not there.'

They were unanimous about Martial, just as they would be on 16 October when he won the Premier League Player of the Month award for September. He beat: Jamie Vardy (Leicester City), Dimitri Payet (West Ham), Odion Ighalo (Watford), Hugo Lloris (Tottenham) and his teammate Daley Blind. It was the first time a United player had won Player of the Month since Robin van Persie in April 2013. That was not all, Anthony also picked up the PFA Fans' Player of the Month prize for September. Not bad for a young player at the start of the season. There was very little to add to the English newspaper headlines: 'an Old Trafford hero is born.'

Chapter 19
Wembley, 17 November 2015

The match was supposed to be a celebration. Anthony had been looking forward to Tuesday, 17 November 2015 for quite some time. But there was no hint of a smile on his lips when the time came to go out onto the Wembley pitch for the friendly between England and France. No smile, but intense emotions visible on his often impassive face. Thousands of French flags were being waved in London's temple of football. It was only four days after the wave of terror attacks that had swept across Paris and up to the gates of the Stade de France, where Les Bleus were preparing for Euro 2016 with a gala match against the world champions, Germany.

On Friday, 13 November, between 9.20 pm and 9.53 pm, three terrorists blew themselves up outside the stadium in Saint-Denis in the Paris suburbs. The match was not stopped to avoid any panic. But the loud bangs, initially taken to be firecrackers, were heard by spectators and players, so much so that Patrice Evra even jumped while he was on the ball. At that moment Anthony was, of course, unaware of the drama that was being played out just a few metres away and, like his teammates, it was only after the match that he found out about the carnage that had unfolded across the French capital. Had he picked up on the charged atmosphere all around him? It is hard to say … as in every game, he was in his bubble and delivered an unflappable, high-level performance during the 2-0 win over the Germans. He was the best French player that night and even, quite simply, the best player on the pitch. Most football websites named him as man of the match and gave him a seven and a half out of ten. It was well deserved because, on his fifth selection for the France team, he threw everything he had at Germany's defence for the 69 minutes he spent on the pitch. The media were unanimous: he was the 'number 1 poison' with 'magic in his feet' when, in injury time at the end of the first half, 'he mystified Rüdiger and Ginter to offer Olivier Giroud the gift of a goal he couldn't miss.'

His runs down the left wing had become a constant feature of the first half of the 2015–16 season. After coming on as a substitute in the two friendlies against Portugal and Serbia in September, Anthony had gone up a level with every appearance for Les Bleus in October. Firstly, there was his third selection against Armenia on 8 October at the Allianz Riviera stadium in Nice. The MU striker made the perfect stand-in for Mathieu Valbuena on the left wing during the last 30 minutes of the game: not long after coming on, he hurtled down the wing but Karim Benzema and Antoine Griezmann failed to take advantage; then there was an assist down the middle for Benzema in the 79th minute that sealed the one-sided match for France 4-0. This first assist while playing in his national colours immediately won over the *France Football* journalist, Patrick Urbini: 'It was a reminder that the Manchester United striker is always very aware of the game, even when he's not facing it, that he is just as comfortable in the middle as on the left, and that he can absolutely complement Benzema. Especially in a quick attacking move when you have to think quickly and see ahead of the others.'

Anthony Martial was starting to become a credible option just eight months from Euro 2016. The good news was that by coming on he had not just caught the eye of the journalists but had also convinced Didier Deschamps to offer him a place in his starting eleven. This was timely because three days after the friendly against Armenia, the French coach took advantage of another warm-up match, this time against Denmark, to try out three new players in attack. In the absence of Benzema (injured after the match against Armenia), Antoine Griezmann, Olivier Giroud and Anthony Martial were ready to take to the pitch at Copenhagen's Parken Stadium; for Giroud and Martial it was a chance to make an impression within sight of the forthcoming tournament to be played on French soil.

Four minutes in and Blaise Matuidi picked out Martial with a deep pass. The Manchester United player passed Simon Kjaer before releasing Olivier Giroud into the area, who sneaked in between Daniel Agger and Riza Durmisi. Giroud's strike went under Kasper Schmeichel's arm and the ball slipped into his goal. 1-0. Anthony's pass was a model of simplicity and accuracy. He and Giroud congratulated each other warmly and sincerely; they had shown a great complementarity and a clear understanding: 'This goal is the perfect example of Anthony having the right mindset,' explains his agent, Philippe Lamboley. 'Some players would definitely have sulked because they weren't playing in the centre-forward position, or would have been selfish instead of laying the ball off for Giroud, one of his competitors in attack … but not him. Anthony knows full well that he has what it takes to play in the centre, but he has this mindset that puts the team first, and this was demonstrated by that assist against Denmark.'

This piece of inspiration was not his only involvement

in the match, however. His performance was complete and he was a part of almost every French attack: fouls, saves, clearances, deflections ... the Danish defence were truly at a loss as to how to stop France's number 11. His understanding with Giroud was passed on to the rest of the team: Anthony combined just as well with the PSG midfielder Blaise Matuidi, and with the third prong in the attack, Antoine Griezmann (Atlético Madrid), who he provided with a goal-scoring opportunity in the second half. The Manchester United player was altruistic but he also knew how to play his own cards and, on several occasions, was close to making the difference on his own, such as in the 63rd minute when he came up against Kasper Schmeichel twice after seeing off Yussuf Poulsen and Simon Kjaer on the left wing. Finally, after a left-footed half volley sailed over the goal, Anthony was taken off in the 87th minute and returned to the bench to compliments from his coach: 'For his first start, Anthony performed well and in a very interesting way. He was on the move a lot and had plenty of rhythm,' said Didier Deschamps a few minutes after his team's 2-1 win over Denmark. 'He took advantage of the time he had on the pitch, which is good. He still has steps to take, but he brings some very interesting things to our team in attack.' The comments from the media were even fuller of praise: 'He was France's most dangerous player. He continued to make the difference and to frighten the Scandinavian defence. Fast, technical and powerful, he has impressive skills for his young age. At this rate, Didier Deschamps soon won't be able to do without him,' predicted Alexandre Jaquin on *RMC Sport*, while Bertrand Volpilhac from *20 minutes* thought he had just witnessed the birth of Les Bleus' future striker: 'To be honest, he was amazing. He was fast, powerful and dribbled well. He made a huge difference on the left wing. If, thanks to this win, Didier Deschamps manages four victories in a row with his team for the first time, there's a good chance that history will remember this match between Denmark and France as the day Martial really kicked off his career as a Bleu.' On the *lequipe.fr* website Anthony was even elected man of the match with 45% of the votes, ahead of Olivier Giroud (30%), who had scored both goals in the French victory! The public had given their verdict on his first senior team start.

The following month, when France were preparing to play their last two matches of the year, Martial found himself on the receiving end of a twist of fate. Everyone had been unanimous about his performance in the match against Denmark but suddenly two of his major competitors in France's strike force, Karim Benzema and Mathieu Valbuena, became embroiled in a court case in which the former was suspected of having blackmailed the latter over an alleged sextape. As a result, neither Valbuena nor Benzema was called up for the two matches on 13 and 17 November against Germany and England. Two unusual matches, the first of which would take place at the Stade de France, watched by his family and friends from Les Ulis. On 13 November 2015 his third assist in five matches would, quite rightly, be eclipsed by the atrocity happening at the same time in Paris, the suicide attacks and shootings claimed by the so-called Islamic State terrorist organisation.

After the match, the team would be kept out of harm's way despondently in their dressing room at the Stade de France; they did not return to Clairefontaine by bus until 4 am. Anthony did not make a statement; he left the older and more well-established players in the team to tell the nightmare story of that evening. During the days that followed, when the announcement of the terrible death toll of 130 and 413 injured came, he would take to social media to express his sadness and emotion. Like many thousands of anonymous supporters, the day after the attack he would post the message 'Pray for Paris' on his Twitter account, followed two days later by an Instagram post of a photo of the Eiffel Tower lit up in red, white and blue accompanied by the comment: '*Elle est magnifique.*'

On Tuesday, 17 November, Anthony found himself on the pitch at Wembley, with plenty of protocol to be observed. He was surrounded by the blue shirts of the France team and not far from his Manchester United teammate Wayne Rooney, who was wearing the captain's armband for the England team. Their duel at either end of the pitch could have been one of the talking points of the match, but the Paris attacks had changed everything. More than a football match, it was a commemoration. The announcement came over the tannoy in both English and French: 'Tonight the people of France and England have come together to demonstrate their unity and solidarity in the wake of the tragic events that took place in Paris on Friday evening.' His highness the Duke of Cambridge, assisted by Prime Minister David Cameron and the France and England team managers, Didier Deschamps and Roy Hodgson, laid a wreath in tribute to the victims and all those affected by the Paris attacks.

'We will now join together to sing *La Marseillaise.*' The moment gave all those in attendance goose bumps. The entire stadium began to sing the anthem written by Rouget de Lisle: '*Allons, enfants de la Patrie, le jour de gloire est arrivé ...*' The lyrics scrolled across the big screens and Anthony sang. It was a unique moment that he would never forget. Such an emotionally charged start to a match would have unsettled many a player. After England's 2-0 win (goals from Dele Alli and Wayne Rooney), Deschamps recognised: 'We weren't in any fit mental or physical state to play.' However, despite being only nineteen, there was one player who did not let the match pass him by: dribbling down the wing, one-on-ones, runs, picking up the ball with his back to goal and rushing along the left sideline … Just as he had been against Denmark and Germany, the kid from Les Ulis had been France's most visible player. But he had not been able to score his first goal for France in his new English kingdom, despite having two good chances. Firstly, from a heavy strike blocked by Joe Hart after the first fifteen minutes, then a fine reflex stop from the substitute keeper, Jack Butland, in the second half. There were some glimmers of promise and hope at such a tragic and turbulent time.

Chapter 20

A Christmas present

Anthony celebrated his twentieth birthday on 5 December 2015. Three days earlier *France Football* had dedicated its cover to him with the title: '*Martial 20 ans et déjà si grand*' [Martial, 20-years-old and already so grown up]. The six-page spread about the kid from Les Ulis began with a long introduction: 'The French player was an unknown in England at the time of his record transfer to Manchester United at the end of August. Three months later, he is among the Red Devils' starting eleven, has been compared to Thierry Henry and is now a permanent fixture with Les Bleus. This is only the beginning of his meteoric rise.' The French weekly recounted how, in just a few games, the ex-Monaco player had conquered England, winning over Van Gaal, the Old Trafford fans and public opinion in the process. There was even a double page of 'Twenty things you need to know' about the number 9 and a map of France and England to pinpoint where other great French champions had been at Martial's age. Zinedine Zidane was serving time with Cannes in Ligue 2 before joining Juventus at the age of 24. Eric Cantona was back at Auxerre after a seven-month loan to Martigues, also in Ligue 2. He would move to Leeds United at 25. Michel Platini had won the Ligue 2 title with Nancy but had yet to play for the French national team. He would go on to join Juventus at 27. Thierry Henry was in the Monaco starting eleven before also making the move to Turin a year later. The only precocious talents were Nicolas Anelka, who was already playing for Arsenal and had scored two goals in a France shirt, and Karim Benzema, with three Ligue 1 titles, seven national team appearances and one goal. He would leave France for Madrid at the age of 21.

This framework demonstrated the measure of Martial's exceptional achievements. He had shattered the notion that a foreign player needed months or even a whole season to adapt to the type of play, rhythm and physical refereeing of the Premier League. Even without really speaking English he had fitted in well into a dressing room full of established star names with season upon season of top-flight football behind them. He had amazed Van Gaal, a coach who always yelled at him in training but usually ended up picking him to start come Saturday. Yet, all that glittered was not necessarily gold. Between late November and early December, criticism of the young hopeful began to bubble up in Manchester and the surrounding area and the voice of dissent was one that demanded to be heard. It was none other than Paul Scholes, 499 appearances and 107 goals for the Red Devils, an English player with one of the largest trophy cabinets in the country: 25 titles including eleven Premier Leagues and two Champions Leagues. The so-called 'Shy Genius' was not satisfied with how the young French player was behaving and the chance he had missed on 25 November in the goalless draw at home against PSV. He blurted out to the *BT Sport* microphones: 'Martial for me has still got a lot to prove goal-scoring wise. He isn't a centre-forward who lives for goals. He's a player who likes to come outside the box, he likes to drift to the left wing. He doesn't look bothered if he misses a chance. He doesn't look bothered if he scores a goal. Maybe they need to go into the transfer market in January.' Scholes even went so far as to suggest that Anthony needed to be sent elsewhere to learn the lesson.

The fans and commentators did not share this opinion. Take Gary Neville, United captain from 2005 to 2010, a pundit and not particularly successful manager at Valencia. He said he had always been impressed with Anthony's explosive impact and explained: 'I was expecting Manchester United to have signed a winger-forward, but what they have actually signed looks like a number nine; someone who can lead the line, and, if he's not scoring goals and not running in behind, provide a point for attacks, and I never expected that.'

Scholes's comments were backed up by none other than Claudio Ranieri, who had direct experience of Martial: 'It is right to make criticism – and Scholes made the right criticism – but it will improve his mind,' said the Leicester City manager. 'His character is very strong, he is young but strong. It is important that he is also intelligent and then he can improve. I think his impact for us was amazing. I have watched him grow a lot since two or three years ago when I bought him from Lyon. Now he is young, but he is a man. Already, three years ago, he knew very well where he will arrive. Because his focus was to achieve a high level of football in the world. And I think he can arrive.'

The boy had plenty to learn, but he would get there, according to the Italian and future King of England. So, why, after so much praise and applause was the new purchase being taken to task by some big names? Quite simply because Van Gaal's game was unconvincing. United were not turning things around, they were not winning and nor were they scoring. His attack was sterile, only six goals in the last nine matches, and four goalless draws in the

Premiership and Champions League. What about Martial? He too was in a dry spell: one goal in the last thirteen games. His last goal dated back to 21 October in Moscow against CSKA. It had been a schizophrenic match for the number 9. In the fifteenth minute a 'stupid reflex', as it would later be defined by the Dutch manager, deflected the ball with his hand in the area. It was the first time he had ever done anything so foolish. It was a clear penalty that was converted by Seydou Doumbia to give the Russians the lead. To make amends, Martial remedied the situation in the 65th minute with a diving header that found the back of the net on the end of a cross from Valencia. He had drawn his team level, scored his fifth goal of the season and his first Champions League goal in a United shirt. Then nothing, in either the Premiership (his last goal dated back to 20 September against Southampton), the Champions League, or the League Cup, in which United were knocked out by Middlesbrough. Anthony had definitely tried, he had kept himself busy, tried to score, defend, worked well with his teammates and sparked the public's anger when Van Gaal replaced him with Fellaini in the return leg against CSKA on 3 November.

But the fact remained that he was not scoring goals at will as he had been in his first few weeks in England. It was reminiscent of Federico Macheda, the Italian who joined United at the age of sixteen, impressed at the end of the 2008–09 season with multiple goals but then, partly due to injury and partly to bad luck, disappeared from the radar and was sold to Sampdoria. There was concern that Martial would go down the same path and end up being a fiasco. On 7 December, the day before the final Champions League Group B match against Wolfsburg, the topic was up for discussion. It was his manager's turn to defend the new arrival: 'I think Martial is very talented but we have to say also that he is just twenty. We have to give him time and that's always difficult when you are playing for a team like United because expectations are very high, but I'm very convinced that he shall continue with his performances and also that he shall score at the right moment again. You cannot expect of a twenty-year-old player coming to the Premier League that he scores every week. I didn't expect it either. When he came he was accelerating in the start of his campaign at Manchester United. I know that and I have to explain it to everybody because he doesn't need that pressure to score every match.'

Martial would find the goal again in Germany. In the tenth minute, prompted by Juan Mata, he fired the ball into the top right corner of Wolfsburg's goal, giving his team the lead. It seemed like a perfect start for United, who had to win in order to progress to the knockout stage, but unfortunately, during the 90 minutes of what turned out to be a crazy game, everything changed. It ended 3-2 to Wolfsburg and the Red Devils said goodbye to the Champions League. Third in the group with eight points: they were heading for the Europa League. It was a real blow for Van Gaal, the club and the fans. Things were no better in the Premier League, where United recorded three defeats and two draws in December. From third in the table, they had slipped to sixth by the end of the year. For Martial, there was the satisfaction of rediscovering his goal-scoring form in the Premier League against Norwich, on 19 December, even if the match ended 2-1 to the Canaries, much to the displeasure of the Old Trafford crowd. Before the match Anthony had been given a nice early Christmas present: the Golden Boy Award 2015, the prize given to Europe's best Under-21 player. Founded in

2003 by *Tuttosport*, the Turin-based sport daily, its prestigious former winners include Lionel Messi, Cesc Fàbregas, Wayne Rooney, Sergio Agüero, Mario Balotelli and Mario Götze. The prize is voted for by leading European sports journalists. Twenty-one of the 30 jurors chose Anthony Martial ahead of Kingsley Coman, the nineteen-year-old French player at Bayern Munich, and Héctor Bellerin of Arsenal. Anthony was the second French player to win the trophy after Paul Pogba, who won it in 2013, and the third United player after Rooney (2004) and Anderson (2008). In 2014, it had been won by Raheem Sterling, formerly of Liverpool and now at Manchester City.

The French Premier League player granted *Tuttosport* the customary photos, on the pitch and in front of a Christmas tree holding the golden ball. He also granted an exclusive interview after a Red Devils warm-up training session at the Carrington centre. When asked to whom he wanted to dedicate the award, Anthony was in no doubt: 'I'd like to dedicate it to our fans, they are incredible, formidable, they travel from anywhere to be near us and no matter where in England or overseas we feel at home because we can always hear them singing and supporting us. The atmosphere at Old Trafford is really unique and when you're a bit tired, they really help you, they shout out your name and that gives you energy. When I'm on the pitch I just focus on my teammates and my opponents, I try to be in a bubble, but it's impossible not to hear the fans chanting.' When asked the eternal question about comparisons with Henry: 'It's an honour to be compared to the great Thierry Henry but I have a duty to remain down to earth. I want to focus on my game and keep growing as a player. Van Gaal told me since last summer to work hard and that's what I'm doing.' And, in a European Championship year there was, of course, a question about the tournament that would be played on French soil. Anthony answered: 'I think it will be a really special Euros. Playing at home is so special and winning would be a dream come true. We have a great team, a very strong team, and we'll play with pride and the privilege of wearing the blue shirt in front of our fans. It will be very special for the whole nation. Pogba, Coman and I make a nice trio, don't we? I think we'll enjoy it …'

Chapter 21
Goals, gossip and love stories

2016 got off to a good start. On Saturday 2 January, United brought a negative run of eight matches without a win to an end against Swansea City at Old Trafford. Martial gave his team the lead with a crushing header on the end of a cross delivered from the right by Bastian Schweinsteiger. The equaliser came from Gylfi Sigurðsson, the Jacks' Icelandic player, who sent a shiver down the spines of the 75,000 fans in the Theatre of Dreams. It was down to Wayne Rooney to save the day with thirteen minutes remaining. Anthony flew down the left wing, went around a defender and guessed correctly with a tight cross from the touchline that was fired home by the captain with a deft touch. Old Trafford could breathe again and Martial could not fail to be pleased with how the year had started. With his eighth goal in 23 appearances in the Premiership, Champions League and League Cup combined, Van Gaal was enthusiastic about his progress on the pitch: 'I am very pleased with how Anthony is developing himself, which is why he always plays, more than I had imagined before,' said the 64-year-old Dutch manager. 'I could not predict that he would play almost every match because when you are twenty years old the rhythm of the Premier League is exceptional, which is why I am very pleased with him.'

It was a shame that cold water would be poured on all

this just eight days later. And it was nothing to do with football.

'Married Anthony Martial's romps with X Factor beauty: Man U ace flew model for sex in Paris. The £36 million striker was given two days off by the club to visit family and friends after his starring role in a 2-1 win last week. But rather than spend time with childhood sweetheart Samantha and five-month-old daughter Peyton, he took Emily Wademan, 24, away for a love tryst.' The exclusive, needless to say, came from *The Sun*. The attack was picked up by all the British tabloids, as well as French websites and gossip magazines. The so-called Voice of the Nation let Emily have her say. The former hostess, Miss Great Britain 2013 finalist and X Factor contestant in 2008 and 2012 gave an in-depth account of their liaison and did not spare any of the juicy details. 'We met after he approached me on social media. He would message me and say: "Send me a picture of your face". He was obsessed with my lips. I would send him pictures and we would just chat about everyday stuff. It might seem stupid but when we first got in touch I didn't do any research, so I just presumed he was single. He sent me pictures of him in an ice-bath after training. He told me he was separated from his wife. It was only when my brother told me later that he had a girlfriend that I realised he was married. But when I asked him he said it was over between them.' Emily explained to *The Sun on Saturday* that they had flown to Paris separately and met up in a five-star hotel in the centre of the French capital. They strolled along the Champs Élysées and Anthony had no problem being photographed with her by fans. They had a candlelit dinner before a wild night of passion. 'He took me for a romantic weekend, but now he has gone back to his wife and child,' concluded the former hostess.

By way of proof, the article appeared next to a selfie of Emily with the United number 9, taken who knows where and who knows when. Whether the tabloid revelations were true or not, they were none too popular with Van Gaal and the Manchester United staff. It was a marked contrast with the image of a young player who said in interviews: 'I'm very homely. After training I like to come and find my girl-friend and daughter, Peyton. I don't go out a lot as I like to stay in. I often go for dinners with my girlfriend and I love to see movies at the cinema but I don't understand them. We go for walks and to the shops but I prefer to stay home.' In short, problems with his English aside, he was the perfect boyfriend and young father. His romance with Samantha Jacquelinet, a 23-year-old French woman, had begun in Monaco. They met, liked each other and became a couple, although they did not get married. Dominique Pandor, Anthony's former Monaco teammate, explains: 'She softened him, helped him focus on his career and to mature. He seems more like a 30-year-old than a twenty-year-old.'

Peyton, Samantha and Anthony's' beautiful baby daughter, was born on 11 June 2015. The new mum posted a photo of her partner in the delivery room cradling the infant in his arms; this would be followed by countless shots of the little girl in coloured pyjamas or a Monaco shirt emblazoned with her father's name. Late August brought the move to Manchester: Samantha welcomed the news with an Instagram post: 'We're starting a new life in England! I love you, your simplicity is what makes you beautiful, *mon Doudou*. We'll never forget Monaco, where our princess was born. Thanks to the fans for all your support.'

On 12 September, after Anthony's United debut, she posted this message: 'Babe, for me you are and will always be my best friend, the best husband ever, a lovely daddy and the best player of the world.' By 17 November the tone had changed. This time it was a rant: 'Instagram isn't Meetic [a French dating website]. According to a study, there are 43.6 million Instagram accounts, around 21.8 million of these belong to men. So, keep going when you see my man's profile, there are still another 21.7 million,' she wrote, next to a photo taken with Anthony, before concluding her tirade with these hashtags: 'My man shows me your messages, girls. You're really keen and some of you are very rude. I love you, Toto.' In November, Samantha's claws came out for the women trying to chat up her Anthony on social media. But in January, there were no Instagram reactions to the revelations in *The Sun* or Emily's confessions. Was it all hype or had she forgiven Anthony?

Life went on and the United number 9 continued to astound the fans with his goals. In the Premier League, he found the back of the net against Stoke City on 2 February, before going on to score on 13 February against Sunderland and on 3 April against Everton. In the quarter-final of the FA Cup he scored against West Ham on 13 March. On 17 March he converted a penalty against Liverpool in the return leg of the last sixteen of the Europa League. The 1-1 draw was worthless: United had lost 2-0 at Anfield and were eliminated from the final European competition in which they were still competing. Which had been his best goal? Without a doubt, the one against Stoke City. The move began in the United penalty area. With a dizzying break, the ball travelled from Michael Carrick to Lingard, from Lingard back to Carrick, from Carrick to Rooney, from Rooney to Matteo Darmian, from Darmian to Mata and then back to Rooney, who picked out Martial on the opposite wing. Anthony kept going into the box and glanced up to check on the position of Jeff Butland, the Stoke keeper, before unleashing a shot into the top corner of his opponents' goal. It was a goal that the French newspapers would immediately compare to Thierry Henry. It was a goal that would eventually win the Premier League's goal of the season award on Twitter, beating Christian Benteke's overhead kick against Manchester United by 57.6 per cent of likes to 42.4 per cent. Which had been his most important goal? With hindsight, the one he had scored against West Ham. In the 83rd minute, Anthony sneaked in behind the Hammers' defence to get on the end of a cross from Ander Herrera and score after a hesitation from Diafra Sakho. It was the goal that evened things up after Dimitri Payet had curved a free kick into De Gea's net from 30 yards out. It was the goal that would see United through to a replay and, as the British papers would claim, save Van Gaal's face and bench. There had also been a historic goal: against Everton on 3 April, Anthony scored United's 1,000th Premier League goal at Old Trafford. He could not have chosen a better moment, given that the South Stand had just been renamed in honour of a Red Devils legend: Sir Bobby Charlton. It was a date the fans would not easily forget. All this led up to Saturday 10 April, a bad day in every sense. That afternoon, United lost 3-0 to Tottenham at White Hart Lane; Anthony failed to shine but was responsible for his team's only shot on goal, which was saved by Hugo Lloris.

A few hours earlier *The Sun* had the boy from Les Ulis in its sights once again. 'Man U ace Anthony Martial dumped by wife Samantha four months after romp with X Factor star Emily Wademan,' was the headline in the tabloid; proof of the separation was apparently offered by the fact that Samantha had stopped following Anthony on Instagram the previous week and had deleted all his photos from her account. The United number 9 was said to have done

the same. *The Sun* added that Martial's agent had suppos-
edly confirmed the break-up. Of course, the paper also
reminded its readers of its exclusive scoop on Anthony's
escapade in Paris with Emily, as if to say that Samantha
had not forgiven her partner in the end and returned to
France. On 4 April, she posted a picture of herself and her
daughter in a pram by a French beach, accompanied by the
curt comment: 'I just want to be with you for life Peyton, I
just want to be a mum.'

That was not the end of it. Far from it. Five days passed
and the gossipmongers were up to their old tricks. In
France this time. 'Anthony Martial bowled Mélanie over
and the feeling was mutual. The French footballer has
found a real shoulder to cry on in the beautiful blonde
after a difficult time,' wrote *Public: Actu et infos des stars et
célébrités*. 'He split from his partner, Samantha, a few weeks
ago. A source close to the reality TV star confirms: "Mélanie
and Anthony have known each other for a while but were
just good friends. They got together very recently. They
suddenly realised how they felt about each other, neither
of them was expecting it. They had cut ties for a long time
when he was still with the mother of his child." So, friends
first, now lovers!'

This unexpected romance, the beautiful love story
described by *Public* immediately became the subject of controversy. Samantha did not hold back, accusing Mélanie of
having sold 'her story with Anthony for fame and money,'
thanking her venomously for having 'broken up her relationship.' Martial's ex asked to be left alone to bring up
her ten-month-old daughter, who was keeping her busy by
waking her up at 4 am. She said she did not want to end up
on television telling her version of the facts, nor would she
accept money for an exclusive interview. She kept her word,

but vicious online accusations and counter accusations flew back and forth between her and the other woman, so much so that it would be best to gloss over them here.

But who is Mélanie Da Cruz, the French striker's new flame? The 25-year-old only child of Portuguese descent was brought up by her mother Armanda after her parents' separation. Her A-levels included history and the classics; after leaving school she earned two vocational qualifications before embarking on training to become a flight attendant. Then she came across reality TV: Secret Story 9 [a *TF1* programme based on the Big Brother format] and the very similar Les Anges 8 gave Mélanie, a big football fan – she supports PSG and Benfica – the opportunity to develop a certain online following. She boasts more than 200,000 followers on Twitter and 799,000 on Instagram. These numbers have helped her acquire sponsors for her posts and to sell the clothes she loves to wear via her website. Online gossip in France has described her as a working girl ready to return to her profession when she's had enough of reality TV. For the time being that is not the case and she has now become a reporter for Mad Mag on the *NRJ12* channel. It was on this programme on 20 June 2016, with Europe in the grip of football fever, that Mélanie Da Cruz confirmed her relationship with the United number 9. Aurélie van Daelen, the presenter, asked:

'We know you're currently sharing your life with the France striker Anthony Martial. You went to the stadium to support him, didn't you? You were photographed there with your mother,' she shows her a snapshot taken at the France Romania game, the first match of Euro 2016.

She then asked: 'Tell us, is it serious?'

'Yes, it's serious. It's going very well,' replied Mélanie, wearing a bright red low-cut dress with her blonde hair in a bun. Aurélie insisted: 'And is all this controversy having an impact on your relationship?'

'Not at all. It's bringing us closer together.' The reality star's shy smile was met with applause and the couple was made official on live TV. By none other than Mélanie herself.

Chapter 22

Anthony *Le Magnifique!*

Excuse me, can I ask you a question?

Of course.

Which scarf has been the most popular this year?

'The Martial one, then Rashford, and then George Best, as always.'

Donovan, who sells United memorabilia, is adamant. So too are the shop assistants at the Old Trafford Megastore: 'The number 9 shirt with his name on the back is the number one, the club's top-selling shirt.' It comes as no surprise then that statistics provided by sporting goods distributors such as Kitbag and Sports Direct have Anthony third in the list of the World's Top Ten Players with the most shirt sales in 2015–16. Just behind Lionel Messi and Cristiano Ronaldo, two giants who have been dominating world football for years. It's a fantastic marketing achievement for a twenty-year-old. But where does this incredible success come from? Behind his stand, pitched right next to a food truck selling enormous hot dogs, Donovan explains everything succinctly: 'In a shit season like this, the fans cling on to anything that gives them hope and Martial, as well as Rashford, have been the only ones to offer a chink of light in what's been a poor and disappointing year.'

It is Sunday, 15 May 2016 the last day of the Premier League season. The weather in Manchester is warm and sunny, a beautiful afternoon for enjoying a football match.

The area around Old Trafford is already packed an hour and a half before kick-off. Thousands of red shirts have invaded the streets next to the stadium, the pubs, fish and chip shops, and burger vans. Fans are eating in the street, bumping into friends, drinking beer and yet more beer, singing their hearts out and buying match programmes, fanzines and scarves, souvenirs of Manchester United against AFC Bournemouth. Travelling fans from India, Norway, Switzerland, Japan and elsewhere take photos and selfies in front of the monument dedicated to the United Legends (George Best, Denis Law and Bobby Charlton). They're killing time waiting for kick-off at three o'clock. They are happy to talk about Martial. Nick, in the middle of a wide street that leads to the East Stand, is selling the *Red News* fanzine, '100% unofficial, for adults only.' He cannot get his words out quickly enough, so keen is he to talk about the number 9: 'He's Manchester United's best player, the player of the year. And the team's top scorer. He scored some important goals when we needed them. And some great goals against Liverpool, Stoke and Everton in the semi-final of the FA Cup. He's wonderful. Definitely. Marcus Rashford? Yes, he's been good at scoring when Martial or Rooney were injured but we need to see him play a bit more with the first team before we can see how good he really is. He needs more experience.'

John, who a few hundred yards further on is noisily selling *United We Stand*, an independent view of the twenty-times Champions of England, shares this opinion: 'He's probably been our best player. If he helps us win the FA Cup on Saturday he will have saved our season. He's the only one who's shone. He's probably the best player we've had since Cristiano Ronaldo.' Andy Mitten, editor of the fanzine, journalist and writer, goes into more detail: 'It's incredible what he's done, particularly when you think how young he is. In his first season in England, he's had to get used to a new country, a new style of play, and he's also suffered, so I've heard, after splitting up from his partner and daughter. He's done great things in a team that hasn't been working, a team with an attack that isn't scoring much, a United that isn't all that much to write home about. But Martial immediately showed what he was capable of. On his debut, at Old Trafford, against our arch rivals, he came on and scored that fantastic goal. What can you say … Wow! Amazing! Even if he'd never played again he would still be a hero for the fans. From that moment on the fans and kids fell in love with Anthony and started buying his shirts and scarves. We needed a player like him at Manchester United. He scored the decisive goal in the FA Cup semifinal with a great moment of form. Just look at his goal at Leicester, or the two he scored against West Ham. He is without a doubt the most dangerous striker we have, he puts fear into our opponents on the pitch. Off the pitch he's a very quiet lad, shy, private, so much so that the club's directors were worried he was ill to start with. His friends in the dressing room are Fellaini and Schneiderlin, but he has a good relationship with all his teammates. No one thinks he's an arsehole; they're all convinced he's a good guy. He has the potential, the talent and the personality to become a world-class player like Cristiano. He could be a Manchester United legend or go to Barcelona or Real Madrid in a few years' time.'

In a few years or a lot sooner given the interest shown by PSG, Real Madrid and other big European clubs? On that subject, Mitten, like most other fans, is prepared to bet. 'PSG is a smaller club with less history, tradition or global audience than Manchester United, which is one of the three biggest clubs in the world. It's obvious that Paris is where Martial was born, but United paid a lot of money for him and they don't need to sell him. There's no financial pressure forcing them to let him go.' 'No, there's no chance of him leaving. He's shown the right attitude. He's enjoyed himself here and is rated by everyone. Any new manager coming in couldn't fail to see Martial's qualities,' claims Andy.

'I would be very surprised if he left, surprised that United would allow a player that's still a work in progress to leave. He could be the successor to Rooney, United's next superstar, like Eric Cantona was. Yes, Martial can be the one to guide us through this awkward transition. He can take us back to the top, to winning the Premier League and the Champions League,' says Philip, convinced, holding his beer in the din of the pub.

It will be his last beer before he sets off for the North West Quadrant. On the way, next to a stall selling scarves and shirts, is a French flag: the blue stripe has a cockerel and the symbol of the French Football Federation, the red stripe has a Manchester United shield, the central white stripe has a picture of the number 9, with the words: 'Anthony Martial *Le Magnifique.*'

Once through the security checks, a lift speeds up to the fifth floor. Seat 127 is a few steps down; it offers great views of the inside of the bowl-shaped Old Trafford. The seating is red, the green pitch is lit up by the sun. There are still three quarters of an hour to go until kick-off and the stands are relatively empty. There's still time for a look at the *United Review*, Manchester United's official programme. Wayne Rooney is on the cover. 'Let's finish on a high' is the title of a long interview in which the captain also has his say on Martial: 'People forget how young Anthony Martial is.

The club bought him so he hasn't come through the academy, but he's still only a really young lad. He's still learning, improving and the same goes for the likes of Memphis Depay, Marcus Rashford, Jesse Lingard, so it's an exciting time for the club. Hopefully they keep improving as players and it'll be a really bright future for Manchester United.'

Let's hear what Steve thinks, sitting two rows away next to Andrew, his father. 'Of course, we're hopeful for the future. We've got some young players with lots of promise. And we've got Martial. He's a great footballer: he can play with either foot, has plenty of pace, is good at dribbling, can get past any opponent and score, and he defends well in the area, plus he has a good header on him. He's also a team player, just look at his assists. He just has to improve his defensive side ...' Steve's father adds a note of criticism to his son's detailed analysis: 'When Rooney came to United he had people like Ruud van Nistelroy and Cristiano Ronaldo in front of him. After Rooney's injury, Martial was on his own and he had too much pressure on him, too much pressure and too much expectation for a twenty-year-old, but it seems as if he's got broad shoulders and he's been able to cope with it very well.'

Someone else gets involved in the conversation, Nicolas, aged seventeen, who has come from Switzerland with his mother for the last match of the season: 'Martial's my favourite player. I followed him in Ligue 1 when he was at Monaco and I already liked him then. When he came here I became his fan. No one here in Manchester knew him but they all love him now.'

They really do love him ... so much so that they have already dedicated a song to him: 'Tony Martial came from France, English press said he had no chance, £50 million down the drain, Tony Martial scores again.' They love him because he has scored seventeen goals (league and cups), equalling the record number of goals for an Under-21 player in their first full season at United. He shares this record with two talented teenagers. In 1967–68, it was set by Brian Kidd, aged only eighteen, in the team managed by Sir Matt Busby. On the day of his nineteenth birthday he scored at Wembley in United's victory against Benfica in the Champions League final. Wayne Rooney tied the record in 2004–05, starting with three goals at Fenerbahçe. He was eighteen and 335 days. Martial still has two matches to go: today against Bournemouth and Saturday, 21 May in the FA Cup final against Crystal Palace, to try to go beyond seventeen goals. Many hope that Anthony will repeat the feat of the nineteen-year-old Cristiano Ronaldo, who, in his first season in a red shirt, opened the scoring with a great header on 22 May 2004 against Millwall at Cardiff's Millennium Stadium, giving the Red Devils their eleventh FA Cup.

Here comes the young French player everyone is talking about, trotting about in the middle of the green rectangle with his teammates. Manchester United are on the pitch for the warm-up. The fans start clapping as they look forward to the 'Battle for Europe', as it had been dubbed by the *Manchester Evening News*. The Red Devils have plenty to play for in this final match of the league season: Champions League qualification. They need to beat Bournemouth and hope that Francesco Guidolin's Swansea will beat Manchester City in the Liberty Stadium. Leicester City miraculously became Champions of England two weeks earlier, and both Tottenham and Arsenal have already booked their tickets for Europe's top competition. There is one game remaining to decide who will take the final top-four berth. Manuel Pellegrini's team only need a draw to secure it: City are on 65 points compared with United's 63, plus they have a better goal difference. Is it mission impossible for the Red Devils? 'I'm convinced we'll do it. I have faith in Swansea,' says Nicolas.

While he is talking a female voice comes over the stadium's loud speakers, announcing a code red security alert. It's 2.40 pm. In the North Stands and Stretford End fans are starting to leave their seats and move towards the exits. Five flights of stairs with their hearts in their mouths. The stewards keep repeating: 'Keep going, keep going. Go as far as you can, don't stop in the car park.' No one knows what's going on. There is no mobile phone coverage. No information, just a mass of people looking back towards the stadium they have just left, as the chants of the Bournemouth supporters still ring out in the distance. Helicopters fly overhead and the stewards form a yellow cordon in front of the entrances. The crowd grows, 50,000 confused people. A father consoles his son, who is in floods of tears. He had come to see his idols and now he's frightened. He is scared and wants to go home as soon as possible. Minutes pass slowly but nothing happens. Then someone says they have cancelled the match. *Sky Sports* confirms it, live. Fans begin returning to Manchester beneath the merciless sun. Streets are blocked, clogged with cars; buses and trams are packed. A beautiful afternoon for football has turned into a nightmare. Someone starts laughing, offering free tickets for the game; others head to a pub to drink and sing. What else is there to do but be philosophical? Later, much later, the reason behind this stadium evacuation, the first in English league history, comes to light. A fake bomb had been discovered in a toilet in the North West Quadrant by Manchester United Staff. That evening, Assistant Chief Constable John O'Hare from Greater Manchester Police would explain: 'The item was a training device, which had accidentally been left by a private company following a training exercise involving explosive search dogs. While this item did not turn out to be a viable explosive, on appearance this device was real.' Tony Lloyd, Mayor of Manchester, described it as an 'unbelievable fiasco.' A terrible mistake that had resulted in chaos and headlines across the world. The match was postponed until 8 pm on Tuesday, 17 May. United were forced to reimburse supporters' tickets and to give fans free entrance to a match that was now pointless as Manchester City had drawn with Swansea and were assured of fourth place and Champions League qualification.

On Tuesday night against Bournemouth, Wayne Rooney, Marcus Rashford and Ashley Young scored, while Chris Smalling put the ball in his own net to pull one back for Bournemouth. The victory saw United finish fifth in the table and opened the doors to the Europa League, small comfort for the Red Devils. Anthony Martial played 84 minutes before being substituted by Young; he failed to score but had created the goal that allowed his captain to make it 1-0. It was his eleventh assist of the season and his third consecutive assist for Rooney.

The FA Cup final took place on 21 May. It was Martial's goal against Everton at Wembley on 23 April that sent United into their first final since 2007, when they lost against Chelsea. It was a sensational goal in the dying moments of an incredible semi-final. After four minutes, the first chance fell to Romelu Lukaku, the Everton striker. It was up to Rooney to head the ball off the line. In the fifteenth minute, Lukaku came again but his weak shot bounced off De Gea's leg. From then on United dominated: in the 21st minute, Martial wasted a half chance from a Lingard pass into the area: his shot flew over the bar. In the 34th minute, Anthony tried again: accelerating down the left wing, he left Muhamed Bešić standing and pulled the ball back into the centre of the area for Fellaini. The former Toffee took it on his left foot and fired the ball past Joel Robles. 1-0. The momentum swung in the second half and Everton were under the cosh. In the 56th minute, David De Gea was the United hero with a world-class save from a penalty taken by Lukaku after a Timothy Fosu-Mensah foul on Ross Barkley in the box. A few moments later, the Spanish keeper saved again from a Barkley free kick outside the area. Martial almost provided Fellaini with a ball to make it 2-0, but the curly-haired Belgian's first touch let him down and the ball was picked up by the Everton defence. Three minutes later the Toffees equalised. A sliding Chris Smalling deflected the ball into his own net from a Deulofeu cross. United did not give up. Martial was the right man, in the right place, at the right time. In the 93rd minute, from the midfield Rooney found Martial on the left wing as the French player signalled with his arms in the air. Anthony tried a one-two with Rashford, ran towards the box, passed to Ander Herrera, who gave him the ball back with his toe, and, once the number 9 got into the box, he left Robles standing. He ran like a madman to the touchline and dived into the arms of the United fans.

It was a goal that impressed Eric Cantona. 'Martial is very mature for his age. I think he's the same kind of player as Ronaldo. Of course Ronaldo is a Brazilian, but he's as strong as him. Martial is skilful, he wants to score goals and he has good vision,' The King told *MUTV*.

The day before the final, Anthony explained: 'It was a very important goal. It was the one that got us through and killed off the match because it was so near to the end. It was

great to go into the crowd and celebrate with the fans.'
He had come to the Carrington training centre dressed
from head to toe in black, in a t-shirt with Invaders written across it in white. It was a good opportunity to send
a message to the fans and to take a look back at his nine
months with United. Anthony said: 'You never know what
happens in the future, but certainly the fans have accepted
me really well and the fact they sing this song about me all
the time shows they're quite happy with me. I have got a
special relationship with them and I'm grateful because
they've always been there for me. From the moment I
arrived they've done their best to make me feel relaxed
and part of things. It has gone some way to helping me in
my overall settling-in period. I just do my best to try to pay
back that support.' He then added: 'I love Manchester and
I love being here and certainly I see myself being here for
a good while yet. I'm certainly happy here.' Then came a
chance to take stock: 'My first season has gone OK, things
have gone relatively well, but I still feel deep down I could
have done better than I have done. I'm hoping to have a
better season next time around. I still consider I'm a player
who has a lot to learn and I'm going to carry on learning
and progressing as an individual.' He even commented on
what Paul Scholes had said in November: 'I'd heard about
that. Goal-scoring is what I do and it's the thing that makes
me most happy. But I'm not the sort of guy who shows that
sort of emotion on the outside too much. But not happy
when I score? Scoring makes me happiest because it's what
it's all about.'

And finally, Martial talked about the FA Cup. He admitted not being 'too aware of the history of the competition,
but I know every trophy you can win has huge importance
and we're going to try to do everything we can to bring the

cup back to Manchester.' He hoped that the atmosphere at Wembley would be 'even better than in the semi-final and we're just going to do everything we can to make sure we win.' After 120 minutes, United would win their twelfth FA Cup at Wembley. Jesse Lingard, who came on for Juan Mata in the 90th minute, was the match-winner. With only ten minutes to go until penalties, he found the perfect strike. Valencia put in yet another cross from the right, only for it to be kept out by the Palace defence ... from the centre of the box the United number 25 took the ball on the volley with the outside of his right foot and rifled the ball under Wayne Hennessey's crossbar. 2-1 and it was all over for Palace. It had been a deathly boring match that only came to life towards the end of the second half, when Jason Puncheon, who had only been on the pitch for six minutes, got the better of De Gea with a left-footed shot from close range that slipped in under the crossbar. Alan Pardew, manager of the Eagles, unleashed a little dance that went viral and would not be easily forgotten. It looked as if it was all over but the Reds reacted. Wayne Rooney, the captain, ran rings around the London team's defence before crossing into the middle of the area. Fellaini, who had hit the bar in the first half, brought the ball down with his chest into the path of Mata, who fired towards the goal. A deflection from a Palace defender helped the ball over the line: 1-1. In extra time, a ten-man United, following Smalling's sending off, found the path to goal with a player who would score his first goal in eighteen matches. What about Martial? It had taken him a while to get into the match and he was not seen galloping down the left wing as he normally would, but he had still been a threat to the Eagles. Unlucky with a header on the end of a Valencia cross, which ended up hitting the bottom of the post, he had managed six shots, more than any other United player, but none had been on target. He had failed to triumph but was delighted with his first trophy in England. For Anthony it could just be the first; for Louis van Gaal, it seemed like it was to be his last with Manchester United.

Chapter 23

Back home

Goodbye Louis van Gaal … Welcome José Mourinho. Two days after their FA Cup victory, Manchester United had already sealed the fate of their Dutch manager and found his successor in the form of the Portuguese coach. The trophy lifted at Wembley was not enough to save Van Gaal after a terrible season in which Anthony had often been forced to keep the team going single-handedly. Mourinho's arrival would give him the opportunity to develop but it was too early to think about that yet … the Manchester striker still had one more goal before the end of the season: winning Euro 2016 with Les Bleus on home soil.

Before beginning his preparation and returning to Clairefontaine, Anthony had a promise to keep. He had agreed to spend an evening at his very first club, the Club Omnisports Les Ulis in the company of another 'local boy made good', Patrice Evra, who would also be part of Didier Deschamps squad for Euro 2016. Two French internationals in the tiny Stade Jean-Marc Salinier ten days before the start of an international tournament was enough to send the town into overdrive.

It is Monday, 23 May 2016 and more than 2,000 people have crowded into the small stand and behind the handrail to celebrate the local celebrities. The kids from Les Bergères, Les Hautes Plaines, Courdimanche and Chantereine only have eyes for Manchester United's new star.

'I'm proud to meet him. I've followed him all season and I'm right behind Manchester United. I hope he'll play well at the Euros,' enthuses an eight-year-old boy hemmed in by a barrier near the official stand where Anthony, dressed from head to toe in black, has just made a brief appearance. Faced by the general euphoria and surging crowd that greets his arrival, he is escorted to the clubhouse. Local officials, such as the town's mayor Françoise Marhuenda, have also come to meet the new champion: 'We already had Thierry Henry and Patrice Evra and now it's Anthony's turn to become a role model for Les Ulis!' Friends, former neighbours and acquaintances are also in attendance, keen to take a minute of their protégé's attention: 'Anthony, can I have a selfie?'; 'Toto, do you remember me?'; 'Anthony, can you sign this for my son?' His family and agent are also here; the Martial clan stands to one side, watching all the excitement with interest and emotion: 'It's very moving, we're proud of what he's done,' says Dorian, Anthony's older brother. 'Our family is respected here and we have a great deal of respect for the city and this club as well.'

A few metres away, Anthony has managed to escape the crowd for a few seconds to fall into the arms of Mimose, his '*seconde maman*', the mother of his best friend who was like a nanny to him. It is a brief moment of intimacy during which the champion struggles to hold back the tears. Mimose gives in to her own and spends a few minutes carried away by the emotion of the reunion: 'When I see him now and I think about that little boy who would come and knock on my door at 6 am to play PlayStation with my son before they went to a tournament, it comes back so strongly.'

Anthony really does seem to have grown up. There is now very little of the timid adolescent who left Monaco at the start of the season to launch his international career.

Although he still has his natural reserve and a hint of shyness, he has developed much more ease and confidence. He is comfortable with his new status.

At around 7 pm, news filters through of Van Gaal's replacement by Mourinho and although Anthony has probably already been told, Manchester United seems far from his thoughts for the time being. He is so happy with his friends and family, and, with a nod to the transfer of power about to take place on the other side of the Channel, he is poised to make his own coaching debut … In the dressing room of the Les Ulis stadium he is greeted by a bench of fifteen Under-13 players from the local club, awaiting their manager for a local gala match. The kids' eyes come out on stalks when Aziz Benaaddane, Anthony's former coach, begins to speak: 'Now guys, as you know, tonight you're going to have the honour of being coached by Anthony. It's only a friendly match, there's nothing at stake, so enjoy yourselves.' Benaaddane turns to Anthony, as if to make him an example, and then goes on: 'You see, when Anthony was twelve and thirteen, he had the same dream you have, of becoming a professional footballer. It was his dream, and a dream like that can't be taken away from you. You can hold on to that dream throughout your life, no matter how old you are. If you believe in it, it's possible! Of course, not everyone in this dressing room will become a professional but it's good to have a dream. It's important when it comes to developing your personality and learning values. When Anthony was at Les Ulis, he trained every day, he wasn't given anything on a plate. Everything he's got today is the result of hard work and respect, thanks to the values passed on to him by his families and the clubs he has played at. Anthony's career is just beginning and we hope he will go as far as possible and win many more titles. You have an opportunity to pay tribute to him tonight by playing well so, enjoy yourselves, encourage each other, motivate each other and don't forget that it's your chance to spend time with someone passionate about football, who loves this club and is kind enough to have come here to give you some advice.'

No one flinches during this two-minute speech delivered by the Les Ulis manager. Anthony backs up his former coach's words with nods of approval. He is also preparing his own speech:

'So, Toto, are you going to say a few words?' suggests Benaaddane. Anthony tries to make his soft voice a little louder: 'I've come here tonight to tell you that at your age it's important to have fun, to enjoy playing with your friends. Work hard at school, that's important, and it will help you to grow. Becoming a professional footballer is a dream that I know you all have if you're here today. So, work hard and you'll get there I'm sure.'

These words are greeted by a round of applause. Anthony is forced to say more by the journalists who have managed to squeeze into the small dressing room and are itching to ask him about his return to the club and the time he spent there as a boy.

'Anthony, what does it mean to you to be here today with these young players at Les Ulis?' begins a journalist from *France Télévision*.

'It feels a bit strange. It's such a long time since I was sitting there on that wooden bench where they are. At their age, I dreamt of becoming Thierry Henry or Patrice Evra. I hope that one of them will have the chance to become a professional player like us one day.'

'How do you explain the success of Les Ulis?' continues another reporter.

'It proves how good the instructors are, they instil real values in us and are very demanding. Les Ulis is my city, my family.'

'What do they think about the Euros in Les Ulis?' asks a local press correspondent.

'I think they'll all be behind us and that we'll win the trophy and bring it back here. The Euros are about to start but for now I've come here to enjoy this moment.'

That's it, or almost. The scene ends with shouts of encouragement sparked off by a coach from Les Ulis: 'Coach Martial has come to help us, let's give him three cheers … Hip, hip, hurray! Louder! Hip, hip, hurray! *Allez Les Ulis … Allez Anthony … Allez Les Bleus!*'

Amid the racket and frenzy of excitement, the dressing room empties as they all come out onto the pitch, where the Under 13s, coached by Anthony Martial are set to take on the Under 12s, coached by Patrice Evra. The records will show that Anthony's coaching debut led to a crushing 3-0 defeat. Despite this, there is plenty of good-natured banter between the two internationals and Anthony proves to be a good loser in the end: 'Pat Evra is a better manager than me!' At 9.30 pm, the match has just finished and the multiple medal-winning judoka and local hero Teddy Riner comes to pay tribute to the two international footballers. Before they all leave, Dorian Martial savours the moment: 'It's been a great day for my brother, a lovely way to unwind with his family and friends.' The eldest of the family concludes: 'Now it's time for the Euros. We hope he'll play a fair amount, have a good tournament and try to carve out a spot for himself in the starting eleven.'

Chapter 24

Missed

Thirteen minutes before utter disappointment, thirteen desperate minutes, thirteen useless minutes, thirteen minutes to change a story that turned on a knife to the heart wielded by Éder, thirteen minutes to fumble a ball in the Portuguese box or to angrily waste a shot at the Portuguese goal, stopped by Pepe, the man of the match. Thirteen minutes on the pitch before tears and sobs on the green grass invaded by moths. Thirteen minutes before the Portuguese go crazy with happiness. Despite the injury to Cristiano Ronaldo they had won their first international trophy in 103 years. They had avenged the semi-final of the 2006 World Cup, when a Zidane penalty deprived them of the final. They had rewritten the defeat in the semi-final of Euro 1984, when Michel Platini scored the winning goal in the 119th minute and sent France through with a 3-2 win. And, after twelve years of waiting, they had erased the angry tears of 4 July 2004, when they lost the final of their home Euros against the incredible Greece in the Estádio da Luz in Lisbon. Thirteen minutes before covering their heads with their *bleu* shirts. Thirteen minutes before climbing the stairs to the stage, shaking the hands of presidents and prime ministers and immediately taking off the losers' medals put around their necks. Thirteen minutes, from the 110th to the 123rd, were all that Didier Deschamps, manager of Les Bleus, granted Anthony Martial in the final of

Euro 2016. He sent him on in place of Moussa Sissoko, who was almost the hero of the night. He sent him on once their fate had almost been sealed. He played his last card, but it was not to be the winning card and it did not see Les Bleus triumph in the sad final at the Stade de France.

They had missed their opportunity. On 10 July 2016, the dream of winning their third European Championship was shattered. The joyous finals of Platini (Euro 1984), Zidane (World Cup 1998) and Trezeguet (Euro 2000) would not be repeated. Les Bleus were favourites ahead of the team managed by Fernando Santos – who had only won one match in 90 minutes against Wales – but in the end the cockerels were beaten in the dying moments by the eternal substitute, Éder, who plays his club football in France, for Lille. They would have to wait for another chance, the World Cup in 2018 ... after all, Les Bleus can count 'on formidable potential, leaders of the future and a young generation that has a desire for revenge,' consoled *L'Équipe*. Martial would also have to wait for another chance. The boy from Les Ulis has the class, talent and potential to be 'a Ballon d'Or winner in three or four years' time,' according to his former coach at OL, Stéphane Roche. He had had an outstanding season with Manchester United but could not break through for Les Bleus. In the second match of the tournament he disappeared from the radar only to reappear for those thirteen sad, lonely and final minutes. Before the start of the Euros many predicted he would be the star of the tournament.

10 June 2016 in Saint-Denis: the curtain was raised on Euro 2016. France and Romania took to the stage. On the left wing was Dimitri Payet, the West Ham player originally from the French island of Réunion; on the right wing, Antoine Griezmann, Atlético Madrid's Petit Prince; and in the centre, Olivier Giroud, the Arsenal star. Martial was on

the bench. Things were not looking good for France in the 65th minute. Bogdan Stancu sent Hugo Lloris the wrong way from the penalty spot, cancelling out Giroud's goal. 1-1 and France had to do it all over again. Deschamps ran for cover. He recalled Griezmann, who had failed to shine, to the bench and sent on Kingsley Coman, the twenty-year-old from Bayern Munich. In the 77th minute, he made another change: he replaced a stuttering Paul Pogba with Martial. A striker for a midfielder, France obviously needed to score. With the number 11 on his back, Anthony went out to the wing, while Payet moved into the centre to dictate the play. The result was more successful. The two young players brought a freshness and vivacity to the team. It was the kid from Les Ulis who tried a low shot in the 81st minute, but Ciprian Tătărușanu, the Fiorentina and Romania goalkeeper, stretched out to block it. It was to be the former Monaco player's only shot on target during the 71 minutes he would spend on the pitch during Euro 2016. In the dying moments, Payet's star soared. The West Ham player came up with a wonderful left-footed shot that made its way into the top corner. The match ended 2-1; Payet had saved France from embarrassment and given them the victory after an agonising match. The Stade de France was in a frenzy; Payet was in tears.

15 June 2016, Marseille, France against Albania. It was Martial's big chance. Didier Deschamps had left Griezmann and Pogba on the bench and picked Martial and Coman in his starting eleven. It was a surprising decision. What were his reasons? There were plenty: it was a stern warning for the Juventus midfielder. The manager expected much from him and in his first 77 minutes Paul had failed to meet those expectations. As for the Atlético Madrid striker, perhaps Deschamps wanted to save him after an endless

season that had ended with defeat in the Champions League final in Milan. The fact was that Les Bleus' number 11 had been handed an opportunity to show what he could do. Without a doubt, it was a chance not to be missed to rise up the ranks of French wingers, where Martial was in fourth behind Payet, Griezmann and Giroud, and on a par with Coman. It was his eleventh cap and his first in a major competition. It was his moment to score his first goal for France. Deschamps had also changed his formation from the usual 4-3-3 to a 4-2-3-1 with Giroud up front, Payet in the control room and his two twenty-year-olds on the wings. It was a great opportunity.

But hopes are not always fulfilled. In the 15th minute, Martial received the ball on the left wing and made it in to the area, but his run was stopped by Ajeti. A few minutes later, he tried again to get into the area through the middle, but the ball ran away from him and he committed a foul. He failed to take advantage of a fine pass from Payet and instead of setting his sights on goal with his left foot, he tried to bring the ball back and was stopped by a defender. He misjudged a pass to Evra, firing it long. He failed to control a high ball from Rami. In short, nothing came off for him and as a result he was forced to relinquish his place to Pogba for the second half. Was it all Martial's fault? No, the whole French team were on the receiving end of boos from the fans in the Stade Vélodrome. They had been unconvincing in attack and no one in the midfield had been able to trigger the speed of the two wingers; in the final minutes of the first half Albania were even dominating play. It had been a disaster and it was definitely not one of Anthony's finest moments. Coman, who had pulled off a Marseille turn and a handful of threatening runs, stayed on the pitch for a few more minutes before being replaced by Griezmann. It was the Petit Prince who turned things around, with the help of Payet: 2-0 and France were flying into the knockout phase.

Martial, however, was no longer flying. After the match, the TV cameras caught him in close-up talking to his father, mother and agent. He looked worried. The following day the newspapers gave their verdict with a three out of ten for his performance. It was hard to imagine anything worse. The most widely-used phrase was '*ratage total*', a squandered opportunity. He was berated for simple technical errors when it came to controlling the ball, misjudged passes, panicking with the ball at his feet, stubbornness when it came to running up against the Albanian defenders, defensive coverage that left a lot to be desired and the fact that he had drifted into the centre too much, depriving Payet of space. The figures spoke for themselves: 67 per cent of passes completed and two out of eight successful one-on-ones. The extenuating circumstances (his age, the fact that he was playing for the first time in a major competition) were not taken into account. David Trezeguet and Thierry Henry, twenty-year-olds with high hopes in the 1998 World Cup, had grabbed with both hands the opportunity given to them by Aimé Jacquet. They had both scored in the second match of the group stage. For the record, France played Saudi Arabia on 18 June 1998, but, be that as it may, the negative assessment of Manchester United's number 9 was harsh and apparently not up for debate.

Or so it seemed, given that Didier Deschamps was no longer prepared to pick him. He was seen warming up along the touchline during the match in Lyon when France went a goal down against the Republic of Ireland, but Griezmann got things back on track and Martial trotted back to the bench. That was it. The French newspapers were convinced. They wrote that, barring any unforeseen injuries, Anthony would see out the rest of the Euros on the bench or in the stands. They described him as the Euros' biggest loser, having been overtaken in the hierarchy of Les Bleus by Coman and Sissoko. In fact, the number 11 did not even appear against Iceland, when the result was overwhelmingly in favour of the French, nor in the semi-final against Germany. Martial the footballer only made an appearance in a training video in which he pulled off an incredible overhead kick to beat Steve Mandanda or with the news that he had twice got the better of Benoît Costil, Les Bleus' third choice goalkeeper, from long range, also in training. Martial the celebrity appeared on social media and gossip websites thanks to his ex Samantha's latest comments about his new flame Mélanie. There was to be no more than those thirteen infamous minutes, which, incidentally, provoked the wrath of Manchester United's fans against Deschamps. 'Not enough time for Martial magic,' they said, with conviction. Who knows whether José Mourinho will agree?

A career in figures

Name: Anthony Martial
Nickname: Toto
Date of birth: 5 December 1995
Place of birth: Massy, Essonne, France
Nationality: French
Parents: Florent, Myriam
Brothers: Johan, Dorian
Partner: Mélanie Da Cruz
Daughter: Peyton
Height: 1.84 m
Weight: 78 kg
Position: forward, winger
Shirt number: 9

Teams

CO Les Ulis (2001–09), Olympique Lyonnais (2009–13),
AS Monaco (2013–15), Manchester United (2015–)

Olympique Lyonnais
First appearance for the first team: 6 December
2012, Europa League group stage match against
Hapoel Ironi Kiryat Shmona
4 appearances, 0 goals

AS Monaco
First appearance for the first team: 30 October 2013,
3rd round of the Coupe de la Ligue against Reims

First goal: 30 November 2013, Ligue 1 match against Rennes
70 appearances, 15 goals

Manchester United
First appearance for the first team: 12 September 2015,
Premier League match against Liverpool at Old Trafford
First goal: 12 September 2015, Premier League match
against Liverpool at Old Trafford
50 appearances, 17 goals

France National Team
Debut: 4 September 2015, friendly against Portugal,
Estádio José Alvalade, Lisbon
12 caps, 0 goals

Titles Won
Manchester United, FA Cup 2015–16

Individual awards
PFA Fans' Player of the Month: September 2015
Premier League Player of the Month: September 2015
Golden Boy: 2015
Manchester United Goal of the Season: 2015–16
Facebook FA Premier League Best Young Player: 2016
Premier League Goal Cup: 2015–16

Bibliography

Books

A.A.V.V., *Olympique Lyonnais*, 2005

Beckham, David, *My Side*, 2004

Benedetti, Richard and Colonge, Serge, *L'Histoire de l'Olympique Lyonnais*, 2013

Best, George, *Blessed, The Autobiography*, 2002

Bitton, Stéphane and Grynbaum, Antoine, *Les secrets du mercato*, 2016

Cantona, Eric, *My Story*, 1994

Descamps, Pierre-Marie and Hennaux, Jacques, *La belle histoire: L'équipe de France de football*, 2004

Duluc, Vincent, *Le cinquième Beatles*, 2014

Duluc, Vincent, *La grande histoire de l'OL*, 2007

Ferguson, Alex, *My Autobiography*, 2014

Ferguson, Alex, with Moritz, Michael, *Leading*, 2016

Goldblatt, David, *The Game of Our Lives: The Meaning and Making of English Football*, 2015

Hindle, Clive, *Only One United: A Personal History of Manchester United*, 2014

Norbert, Siri, *ASMFC: AS Monaco Football Club*, 2008

Rooney, Wayne, *My Decade in the Premier League*, 2012

Winter, Henry, *Fifty Years of Hurt: The Story of England Football and Why We Never Stop Believing*, 2016

White, Jim, *Manchester United: The Biography*, 2009

Newspapers
UK
The Times
The Guardian
The Independent
Daily Mirror
Daily Star
Daily Telegraph
The Sun
Manchester Evening News

France
Le Monde
Libération
Le Figaro
L'Équipe
Le Parisien
Le Journal de Dimanche
Le Progrès
Nice-Matin
Monaco-Matin
20 minutes
Agence France-Presse

Italy
Tuttosport

Magazines
FourFourTwo (England)
World Soccer (England)
France Football (France)
So Foot (France)
United We Stand (England)

Red News (England)
United Review (England)

TV/Radio
BBC (England)
Sky Sports (England)
France Télévision
Canal+ (France)
TF1 (France)
NRJ12 (France)
OLTV (France)
AS Monaco TV (France)
Radio Montecarlo
RTL radio (France)
MUTV (England)
TalkSPORT (England)
BT Sport (England)

Websites
www.fifa.com
www.uefa.com
www.uliscofootball.fr
www.ville-gif.fr
www.olweb.fr
www.asmonaco.com
www.manutd.com
www.footballleaks.es
www.footmercato.net
www.public.fr
www.fff.fr
www.anthonymartial-official.com
www.facebook.com/AnthonyMartialAM9

Acknowledgements

Thanks to Anthony Martial, his mother Myriam, his father Florent and his brothers Dorian and Johan. Thanks to his agent Philippe Lamboley, his friends 'Titoune' and 'Pépère', and to his second mother 'Mimose'. Thanks to the city of Les Ulis, its mayor Françoise Marhuenda, its deputy mayor Paul Loridant and its inhabitants. Thanks to CO Les Ulis, its directors, instructors and players Jean-Michel Espalieu, Aziz Benaaddane, Mahamadou Niakaté, Wally Bagou, Gaye Niakaté (Musik 91) and the children at the club.

Thanks to the invaluable taxi driver Sébastien Torres.

Thanks to OC Gif Football club and its directors: Pierre Durand and Yves Invernizzi.

Thanks to the directors, instructors and players at Olympique Lyonnais: Florian Maurice, Rémi Garde, Stéphane Roche, Gérard Bonneau, Robert Valette, Armand Garrido, Joël Fréchet, Jean-Baptiste Grégoire, Cyrille Dolce, David Pavageau, Alain Rinaudeau, Patrick Berthet, Mathieu Boyer, Zakarie Labidi, Pierre Ertel, Romaric N'Gouma, Mour Paye and Farès Bahlouli, and to its supporters Franck (@lokakilOL) and Olivier (@goneacademie).

Thanks to the directors, instructors, players and journalists at AS Monaco: Éric Abidal, Anthony De Freitas, Dominique Pandor, Jérémy Toulalan, Mounir Obbadi, Samir Kouakbi, Mathieu Faure and Fabien Pigalle.

Thanks to the coaches at the Fédération Française de Football: Francis Smerecki, Jean-Claude Giuntini and Willy Sagnol.

Thanks to James Taylor, Andy Mitten, Duncan Heath, Philip Cotterell, Robert Sharman, Michael Sells, Laura Bennett, Laure Merle d'Aubigné and Roberto Domínguez.

Dedicated to our four champions
Mathieu, Elisa, Olmo and Lorenzo.

To our budding stars
Arthur, Juliette, Jules, Colin, Tom, Louis and Méline.

To Céline, my priceless proofreader.

To Elvira.

To Alda and Tullio.